PENGUIN

LION

Lion

SAROO BRIERLEY
WITH LARRY BUTTROSE

PENGUIN BOOKS

PENGUIN BOOKS

UK | USA | Canada | Ireland | Australia
India | New Zealand | South Africa

Penguin Books is part of the Penguin Random House group of companies
whose addresses can be found at global.penguinrandomhouse.com.

Penguin
Random House
UK

Previously published as *A Long Way Home*
First published in Australia by Viking, a division of Penguin Group (Australia) 2013
First published in Great Britain in Penguin Books 2014
This edition published 2016

001

Typeset by John Canty © Penguin Group (Australia)
Printed in Great Britain by Clays Ltd, St Ives plc

A CIP catalogue record for this book is available from the British Library

ISBN: 978-1-405-93411-4
OM EDITION ISBN: 978-1-405-93197-7

www.greenpenguin.co.uk

MIX
Paper from
responsible sources
FSC   FSC® C018179
www.fsc.org

Penguin Random House is committed to a
sustainable future for our business, our readers
and our planet. This book is made from Forest
Stewardship Council® certified paper.

For Guddu

CONTENTS

PROLOGUE

They've gone.

I've been thinking about this day for twenty-five years. Growing up half a world away, with a new name and a new family, wondering whether I would ever see my mother and brothers and sister again. And now here I am, standing at a door near the corner of a run-down building in a poor district of a small, dusty town in central India – the place I grew up – and no-one lives there. It's empty.

The last time I stood here I was five years old.

The door, its hinges broken, is so much smaller than I remember it as a child – now I would have to bend over to fit through it. There's no point in knocking. Through the window, as well as some gaps in the familiar crumbling brick wall, I can see into the tiny room my family shared, the ceiling only a little higher than my head.

This was my worst fear, so paralysing that I suppressed it almost completely – that once I finally found my home, after years of searching, my family wouldn't be in it.

Not for the first time in my life, I'm lost and I don't know what to do. This time I'm thirty, I've got money in my pocket and a ticket home, but I feel just like I did on that railway platform all those years ago – it's hard to breathe, my mind is racing and I wish I could change the past.

Then the neighbour's door opens. A young woman in red robes comes out of the better maintained flat next door, holding a baby in her arms. She's curious, understandably. I look Indian, but my Western clothes are probably a little too new, my hair carefully styled – I'm obviously an outsider, a foreigner. To make matters worse, I can't speak her language, so when she speaks to me, I can only guess that she's asking me what I want here. I remember barely any Hindi and I'm not confident about how to pronounce the little I do know. I say, 'I don't speak Hindi, I speak English,' and I'm astonished when she responds, 'I speak English, a little.' I point at the abandoned room and recite the names of the people who used to live there – 'Kamla, Guddu, Kallu, Shekila' – and then I point to myself and say, 'Saroo.'

This time the woman remains silent. Then I remember

something Mum gave me back in Australia, for just this situation. I scrabble around in my daypack and pull out an A4 page with colour photographs of me as a child. Again I point to myself, and then say 'little' as I point to the boy in the photographs. 'Saroo.'

I try to remember who lived next door to us when this was my home. Was there a little girl who could now be this woman?

She stares at the page, then at me. I'm not sure if she understands, but this time she speaks, in hesitant English.

'People . . . not live here . . . today,' she says.

Although she is only confirming what I know, to hear her say it aloud hits me hard. I feel dizzy. I'm left standing there in front of her, unable to move.

I've always known that even if I managed to find my way back here, my family might have moved. Even in my short time with them, they had moved here from another place – poor people often don't have much say in where they live, and my mother used to have to take whatever work she could get.

These are the thoughts that start coming out of the box I've put them in. The other possibility – that my mother is dead – I jam back inside.

A man who has noticed us approaches, so I start my mantra over again, reciting the names of my mother, Kamla, my brothers, Guddu and Kallu, my sister, Shekila, and me, Saroo. He is about to say something when another man wanders up and takes over. 'Yes? How can I help?' he says in clear English.

This is the first person I've been able to talk to properly since I arrived in India, and my story comes tumbling out quickly: I used to live here when I was a little boy, I went off with my brother and got lost, I grew up in another country, I couldn't even remember the name of this place, but now I've found my way back here, to Ganesh Talai, to try to find my mother, my brothers and my sister. Kamla, Guddu, Kallu, Shekila.

He looks surprised at the story and I recite the family names yet again.

After a moment, he says, 'Please wait here. I'll be back in two minutes.'

My mind races with possibilities – what's he gone to get? Someone who might know what happened to them? An address, even? But has he understood who I am? I don't have to wait long before he's back. And he says the words I'll never forget: 'Come with me. I'm going to take you to your mother.'

1

REMEMBERING

When I was growing up in Hobart, I had a map of India on my bedroom wall. My mother – my adoptive mother, Mum – had put it there to help me feel at home when I arrived from that country at the age of six to live with them, in 1987. She had to teach me what the map represented – I was completely uneducated and don't think I even knew what a map was, let alone the shape of India.

Mum had decorated the house with Indian objects – there were some Hindu statues, brass ornaments and bells, and lots of little elephant figurines. I didn't know then that these weren't normal objects to have in an Australian house. She had also put some Indian printed fabric in my room, across the dresser, and a carved wooden puppet in a brightly coloured outfit. All these things were sort of familiar, even if I hadn't seen anything exactly like them before. Another adoptive parent might have made the decision that I was young enough to start my life in Australia with a clean slate and could be brought up without much reference to where I'd come from. But my skin colour would always have given away my origins, and anyway, she and my father chose to adopt a child from India for a reason.

The map's hundreds of place names swam before me in my childhood. Long before I could read them, I knew that the immense V of the Indian subcontinent was a place teeming with cities and towns, with deserts and mountains, rivers and forests – the Ganges, the Himalayas, tigers, gods! – and it came to fascinate me. I would stare up at the map, lost in the thought that somewhere among all those names was the place I had come from, the place of my birth. I knew it was called 'Ginestlay', but whether that was the name of a city, or a town, or a village, or maybe even a street – and where to start looking for it on that map – I had no idea.

I didn't know for certain how old I was, either. Although official documents showed my birthday as 22 May 1981, the year had been estimated by Indian authorities and the date was the day I had arrived at the orphanage from which I had been offered up for adoption. An uneducated, confused boy, I hadn't been able to explain much about who I was or where I'd come from.

At first, Mum and Dad didn't know how I'd become lost. All they knew – all anyone knew – was that I'd been picked off the streets of Calcutta, as it was still known then, and after attempts to find my family had failed I had been put in the orphanage. Happily for all of us, I was adopted by the Brierleys. So to start with, Mum and Dad would point to Calcutta on my map and tell me that's where I came from – but in fact the first time I ever heard the name of that city was when they said it. It wasn't until about a year after I arrived, once I'd made some headway with English, that I was able to explain I didn't come from Calcutta at all – a train had taken me there from a train station near 'Ginestlay', which might have been called something like 'Bramapour', 'Berampur' . . . I wasn't sure. All I knew was that it was a long way from Calcutta and no-one had been able to help me find it.

Of course, when I first arrived, the emphasis was on the future, not the past. I was being introduced to a new life in a very different world from the one I'd been born into, and my new mum and dad were putting a lot of effort into facing the challenges that brought. Mum didn't worry too much about my learning English immediately as she knew it would come through day-to-day use. Rather than trying to rush me into it, she thought it was far more important at the outset to comfort and care for me, and gain my trust. You don't need words for that.

She also knew an Indian couple in the neighbourhood, Saleen and Jacob, and we would visit them regularly to eat Indian food together. They would speak with me in my own language, Hindi, asking simple questions and translating instructions and things Mum and Dad wanted me to know about how we'd live our life together. Coming from a very basic background, I didn't speak much Hindi either, but being understood by someone was a huge help in becoming comfortable about my new surrounds. Anything my new parents weren't able to communicate through gestures and smiles we knew Saleen and Jacob could help us with, so we never got stuck.

As children do, I picked up my new language quite quickly. But at first I spoke very little about my past in India. My parents didn't want to push me to talk about it until I was ready, and apparently I didn't show many signs that I gave it much thought. Mum remembers a time when I was seven, when out of the blue I got very distressed and cried out, 'Me begot!' Later, she found out I was upset that I had forgotten the way to the school near my Indian home, where I used to walk to watch the students. We agreed then that it probably didn't matter anymore. But deep down, it did matter to me. My memories were all I had of my past, and privately I thought about them over and over, trying to ensure I didn't 'beget'.

In fact, the past was never far from my mind. At night,

memories would flash by and I'd have trouble calming myself so I could sleep. Daytime was generally better, with lots of activity to distract me, but my mind was always busy. As a consequence of this and my determination not to forget, I have always recalled my childhood experiences in India clearly, as an almost complete picture – my family, my home and the traumatic events surrounding my separation from them have remained fresh in my mind, sometimes in great detail. Some of these memories were good, and some of them bad – but I couldn't have one without the other, and I couldn't let them go.

My transition to life in another country and culture wasn't as difficult as one might expect, most likely because, compared to what I'd gone through in India, it was so obvious that I was better off in Australia. Of course, more than anything I wanted to find my mother again, but once I'd realised that was impossible I knew I had to take whatever opportunity came my way to survive. Mum and Dad were very affectionate, right from the start, always giving me lots of cuddles and making me feel safe, secure, loved and, above all, *wanted*. That meant a lot to a child who'd been lost and had experienced what it was like when no-one cared about him. I bonded with them readily and very soon trusted them completely. Even at the age of six (I would always accept 1981 as the year of my birth), I understood that I had been awarded a rare second chance. I quickly became Saroo Brierley.

Now I was safe and secure in my new home in Hobart, I thought perhaps it was somehow wrong to dwell on the past – that part of the new life was to keep the old locked away – so I kept my night-thoughts to myself. I didn't have the language to explain it at first, anyway. And to some degree I also wasn't aware of how unusual my story was – it was upsetting to me, but I thought it was just the kind of thing that happened to people. It was only later, when I began to open up to people about my experiences, that I knew from their reactions it was out of the ordinary.

Occasionally the night-thoughts would spill over into the day. I remember Mum and Dad taking me to see the Hindi film *Salaam Bombay*. Its images of the little boy trying to survive alone in a sprawling city, in the hope of returning to his mother, brought back disturbing memories so sharply that I wept in the dark cinema, my well-meaning parents unaware of the cause.

Even sad music of any kind (though particularly classical) could set off emotional memories. Seeing or hearing babies cry also affected me strongly, but somehow the most emotional thing was seeing other families with lots of children. I suppose that, even in my good fortune, they reminded me of what I'd lost.

But slowly I began talking about the past. Only a month or so after my arrival, I described to Saleen my Indian family in outline – mother, sister, two brothers – and that I'd been separated from my brother and become lost. I didn't have the resources to explain too much, and Saleen gently let me lead where I wanted to go, rather than pressing me. Gradually, as my English improved, I told Mum and Dad a few more things, like the fact that my father had left the family when I was very little. Most of the time, though, I concentrated on the present: going to school, making friends and discovering a love of sport.

Then, one wet weekend just over a year after I'd arrived in Hobart, I surprised Mum – and myself – by opening up about my life in India. I'd probably come to feel more settled in my new life and had some more words to put to my experiences. I found myself telling her more than ever before about my Indian family: about how we were so poor that we often went hungry, or how my mother would have me go around to people's houses in the neighbourhood with a pot to beg for any leftover food. It was an emotional conversation and Mum held me close. She suggested that together we draw a map of the place I was from, and as she drew I pointed out where my family's home was on our street, which way you went to walk to the river where all the kids played, and where the bridge was under which you walked to get to the train station. We traced the route with our fingers and then drew the home's layout in detail. We put in where each member of my family slept – even the order in which we lay down at night. We returned to the map and refined it as my English improved. But in the whirl of memories brought on by first making that map, I was soon telling Mum about the circumstances of my becoming lost, as she looked at me, amazed, and took notes. She drew a wavy line on the map, pointing to Calcutta, and wrote 'a very long journey'.

A couple of months later, we took a trip to Melbourne to visit some other kids who had been adopted from the same Calcutta orphanage as me. Talking enthusiastically in Hindi to my fellow adoptees inevitably brought back the past very vividly. For the first time, I told Mum that the place I was from was called Ginestlay, and when she asked me where I was talking about, I confidently, if a little illogically, replied, 'You take me there and I'll show you. I know the way.'

Saying aloud the name of my home for the first time since arriving in Australia was like opening a release valve. Soon after that, I told an even more complete version of events to a teacher I liked at school. Over an hour and a half, she wrote notes too, with that same amazed expression. Strange as I found Australia, for Mum and my teacher, hearing me talk about India must have been like trying to understand things that had occurred on another planet.

*

The story I told them was about people and places I'd turned over in my mind again and again since I arrived, and which I would continue to think about often as I grew up. Not surprisingly, there are gaps here and there. Sometimes I'm unsure of details, such as the order in which incidents occurred, or how many days passed between them. And it can be difficult for me to separate what I thought and felt then, as a child, from what I've come to think and feel over the course of the twenty-six years that followed. But although repeated revisiting, searching the past for clues, might have disturbed some of the evidence, much of my childhood experience remains vivid in my memory.

Back then, it was a relief to tell my story, as far as I understood it. Now, after the life-changing events sparked two years ago, I am excited by the prospect that sharing my experiences might inspire hope in others.

2

GETTING LOST

First of all, I remember days spent watching over my baby sister, Shekila, her grubby face smiling up at me as we played peeka-boo. And I remember long, warm nights during the hot months of the year, when my family would join the others with whom we shared the house and gather together outside in the court-yard, while someone played the harmonium and others sang. I had a real sense of belonging and wellbeing on those nights. The women would bring out bedding and blankets, and we would all huddle together, gazing up at the stars, before closing our eyes in sleep.

That was in our first house, where I was born, which we shared with another Hindu family. Each group had their own side of a large central room, with brick walls and an unsealed floor of cowpats, straw and mud. It was very simple, but certainly no *chawl*, those warrens of slums where the unfortunate families of the megacities like Mumbai and Delhi find themselves living. Despite the closeness of the quarters we all got along. My memories of this time are some of my happiest.

My mother was a Hindu and my father a Muslim – an unusual marriage at the time, and one that didn't last long. My father spent very little time with us – I later discovered he had taken a second wife – and so my mother raised us by herself. Although we weren't brought up as Muslims, my mother moved us to the Muslim side of town, where I spent most of my childhood. She was very beautiful, slender, with long, lustrous hair – I remember her as the loveliest woman in the world. As well as my mother and my baby sister, there were also my older brothers, Guddu and Kallu, whom I loved and looked up to.

In our second home we were by ourselves, but in more cramped quarters. Our flat was one of three on the ground level of a red brick building, and so had the same cowpat and mud floor. Again a single room, it had a little fireplace in one corner and a clay tank in another, with water we'd drink and sometimes wash with. There was a single shelf where we kept our sleeping blankets. The structure was always falling apart a little – my brothers and I would sometimes pull out a brick and peer outside for fun, before putting it back in place.

Our town was generally hot and dry, except during the heavy rains of the monsoon. A range of large hills in the distance was the source of the river that ran past the old town walls, and in the monsoon, the river would break its banks and flood the surrounding fields – we used to wait for the river to fall back after the monsoon rains stopped, so we could get back to trying to catch little fish in more manageable waters. In town, the monsoon also meant the low railway underpass filled with water from the stream it crossed and become unusable. The underpass was a favourite place to play, despite the dust and gravel that sometimes rained down on us when a train crossed.

Our neighbourhood of the town was very poor. When I was running along its broken and unpaved streets, it housed the town's many railway workers, and to the more wealthy and highborn citizenry of the town it was literally on the wrong side of the tracks. There wasn't much that was new – some of the buildings were tumbling down. Those who didn't live in communal buildings lived in tiny houses like we had, one or two rooms down narrow, twisting alleyways, furnished in the most basic way – a shelf here and there, a low wooden bed and a tap over a drain, perhaps.

Apart from us kids, the streets were full of cows wandering around, even in the town centre, where they might sleep in the middle of the busiest roads. Pigs slept in families, huddled together on a street corner at night, and in the day they would be gone, foraging for whatever they could find. It was almost as if they worked nine to five, and clocked off to go home and sleep. You wouldn't know if they belonged to anyone – they were just there. There were goats too, kept by the Muslim families, and chickens pecking in the dust. Unfortunately, there were also lots of dogs, which scared me – some were friendly, but many were unpredictable or vicious. I was particularly afraid of dogs after I was chased by one, snarling and barking. As I ran away, I tripped and hit my head on a broken tile sticking up from the old pathway. I was lucky not to lose an eye, but got a bad gash along the line of my eyebrow, which a neighbour patched up with a bandage. When I'd finally resumed my walk home, I ran into Baba, our local holy man, and he told me never to be afraid of dogs – that they would only bite you if they felt you were scared of them. I tried to keep that advice in mind, but remained nervous around dogs on the street. I knew from my mother that some dogs had a deadly disease that you could catch from them, even if they didn't do worse than nip you. I still don't like dogs, and I've still got the scar.

After my father left, my mother had to work to support us. Soon after Shekila's birth, she went off to work on building sites, carrying heavy rocks and stones on her head in the hot sun, six days a week, from morning until dusk. It meant I didn't see very much of her. Often she had to go to other towns for work and could be away for days at a time. Sometimes we would only see her a couple of times a week. And still she couldn't earn enough money to provide for herself and four children. To help make ends meet, when Guddu was around ten, he took a job washing dishes in a restaurant. Even then, we often went hungry. We lived one day at a time. There were many occasions when we begged for food from neighbours, or begged for money and food on the streets by the marketplace and around the railway station, but somehow we managed a subsistence, living day-to-day and hand-to-mouth. Everyone used to go out at the start of the day and get whatever they could, be it money or food, and at the end of each day we would return, put whatever we had managed to find on the table, and everyone would share. I remember feeling hungry most of the time, but oddly enough I wasn't too distressed by it. It became part of life and I accepted it. We were very skinny children, with blown-up stomachs from gas and no food. We were probably malnourished, but then so were poor children all across India, so it was nothing out of the ordinary.

Like a lot of kids in the neighbourhood, my brothers and I got creative about finding things to eat. Sometimes it was as simple as throwing stones at mangoes up in someone's tree, trying to knock one down. But other times we were more adventurous.

Walking home one day, we decided to take a back way through the fields and came across a large hen house, around fifty metres long. Armed guards were on duty but Guddu thought we could safely get our hands on some eggs, so we made a plan. We would stay hidden until the guards went on a tea break, then I would go into the hen house first, being shorter and harder to spot, and Guddu and Kallu would follow. Guddu told us to roll our shirts up inside out so that they could serve as little baskets. We were to collect as many eggs as quickly as we could, then run out and go straight back home.

We watched from a hideout until the guards' break, when they went to sit with the shed workers, eating rotis and drinking chai. There was no time to waste. I was first inside and started grabbing eggs. Guddu and Kallu followed and did the same. But the chickens became disturbed by our presence and started squawking loudly, alerting the guards. We dashed straight back out as the guards ran towards the shed, only about twenty metres from us. Guddu yelled, 'Run for it!' and we split up and bolted. We were a lot faster than the guards, and luckily they chose not to shoot at us. After sprinting for a few minutes I realised I'd given them the slip and walked the rest of the way home.

Unfortunately, the act of running had not been kind to my eggs, and of the nine I'd collected only two remained intact – the rest were dripping down my shirtfront. My brothers had beaten me home and my mother had the fry pan on the flame. Between us we had ten eggs left – enough to feed us all. I was ravenous as I watched my mother give the first batch to Shekila and I couldn't help myself – I nabbed a fried egg from my sister's plate and ran out the door, ignoring her ear-splitting cry of protest.

On another occasion, I woke early feeling very hungry and found there was nothing to eat in the house. I remembered having noticed a field of ripening tomatoes nearby and went out determined to lay my hands on some. It was cool in the early morning air and I still had my sleeping blanket wrapped around me. When I reached the field, I squeezed in through a gap in the barbed-wire fence and within moments I was picking tomatoes, eating some on the spot, savouring their soft flesh. But then I heard a whistle blow loudly and saw a group of five or six older boys running quickly towards me across the field. I dashed back to the fence, and, being little, managed to squeeze through an opening I knew would be too small for them. My prized red blanket got snagged on the barbed wire, and with the boys bearing down on me I had no choice but to leave it behind. When I got home my mother was happy I had brought some tomatoes to eat, but furious I had lost my blanket in the process. She didn't beat me like a lot of parents did, though; she never raised a hand to any of us.

Another run-in involving food almost cost me my life. I accepted a job ferrying ten large watermelons across the town's main street for a man with a stall in the town market. He offered me a little money and I hoped he might add a slice of watermelon when I was done. But the watermelons were very large and I was still small, and, struggling with the first one, I wasn't able to keep track of the heavy traffic. The next thing I knew, I was lying on the tarred road, bleeding from the head, with the watermelon next to me crushed into crimson pulp. I was lucky my head had not been crushed in the same way, as I'd been struck by a speeding motorcycle and gone under its wheel. My leg was also injured. The rider took pity on me and gave me a lift home, and I limped into my house. My mother was horrified and took me straight to a doctor, who bandaged my injuries. I don't know how she paid for it.

As they grew up, my brothers spent more time away from Ginestlay, searching for new hunting grounds and sleeping away from the house in railway stations and under bridges. Sometimes the holy man, Baba, would look after Shekila and me at the mosque, or he would take me fishing in the river with his long bamboo stick and line. Otherwise, we would be in the care of other families who lived nearby, or with Guddu in the restaurant where he scrubbed pots and pans at a tub.

*

Harsh as all this sounds, I think we were reasonably happy, although of course we would have wished for things to be different. Often, first thing in the morning, I would go and hang around by the gates of the local school as the children entered in their uniforms, and I would stare inside, wishing I could be a pupil there like them. But we couldn't afford for me to be sent to school. It made me a bit shy, because it was obvious I had no education. I couldn't read or write, and didn't know many words – I spoke poorly and had trouble communicating.

The person I was closest to was my baby sister, Shekila. After a certain age, I was responsible for her welfare. My duties were to wash and feed her, and watch over her. Shekila and I used to sleep in the same bed, and when we woke I would fetch her whatever breakfast I could find. We used to play together: peekaboo and hide and seek. Shekila was so tiny and beautiful. She loved being with me and followed me everywhere, and I protected her and was always on alert to hear if anyone had mistreated her. Shekila was my main priority, as much as a very young child can have a sense of that sort of responsibility. Although Guddu was older, Kallu played a similar role with him. As Guddu had taken on a few jobs at different times to help with the family income, Kallu took care of him as one of our breadwinners – the younger brother would ensure that the elder was getting enough to eat and that if he stayed away from the home he had a safe place to sleep. So with no father around, and our mother often away working, we took care of each other.

For the most part, I stuck to the boundaries of the house and its courtyard. I spent long days sitting on the earthen floor alone, idly listening in on conversations and watching life go on around me, while Shekila slept inside. Sometimes the local townsfolk who kept an eye on us would let me go off and find wood for cooking, and I would haul it back and stack it by the side of the house. I also occasionally earned a paisa or two – enough for a lollipop – by helping the local storekeeper with his deliveries of wooden planks. He'd have me stack them in the pen by the store's front door. But mostly I simply sat alone in that courtyard. We had no TV or radio. There were no books or newspapers, although, of course, I couldn't have read them anyway. It was a simple, basic existence.

Our diet was basic as well: roti bread, rice and daal, sometimes with a few vegetables tossed in, if we were lucky. There was fruit grown in our area, but that was a luxury and most of it was sold off for cash. There weren't many trees around that we could pilfer fruit from. Like the town's vegetable plots, they were well guarded. We learned to live with hunger, as it was always there.

In the afternoons, kids would come by after school and I was allowed to go off and play with them. Sometimes we'd play cricket on whatever patch of bare earth we could use. I also loved to chase butterflies, or glowbugs when it got darker. Flying kites was another favourite pastime. The kites were very simple – sticks and paper – but to own even a basic kite required a little money. So if I wanted a kite, I'd try to spot one stuck in a tree and climb up and get it, no matter how dangerous it was. We conducted some exciting kite dogfights, for which we would stick sand to our kite's string, giving it an abrasive cutting edge. We would try to cut the string of the other's kite as it flew. Kids played marbles too, but again, you needed money to get a marble to start with.

I didn't really have any close friends – maybe it was because of our having moved neighbourhoods, or perhaps a general mistrust of those I didn't already know well – so I hung out as much as possible with my brothers, whom I adored.

As I got a bit older, I was given more leeway outside the house and was allowed to start playing with kids further away. Sometimes I'd leave Shekila at the house for a while, knowing she could safely pass the time by herself while I was out – I'm sure this is illegal in the West, but in my town it wasn't uncommon when parents had other things to do, and I'd been left like that many times myself so I didn't feel guilty about it.

Like any kid, to begin with I stayed close to home, so that if anything bad happened I could run down this or that street, take a quick turn, and be home. Eventually, though, I started venturing as far as the town centre. Or my brothers and I would go down to the river below the dam wall, a long walk away, beyond the edge of town. We'd watch fishermen using nets to catch fish.

By this time, Guddu and Kallu were about fourteen and twelve, and spending very little time at home. I didn't see them more than two or three times a week. They were mostly living off their wits, scouring the streets for whatever they could find to subsist on and sleeping nights in railway stations, where they sometimes earned food or money for sweeping. Most of the time they stayed at another town a few stops down the train line, about an hour away. They would tell me Ginestlay was no good, so they were going to a place called something like 'Berampur' – I couldn't quite remember its name – where it was easier to find money and food. And they had started making friends there, all of them getting around by jumping on and off trains.

When I was about four or five, occasionally my brothers would take me along with them. If a conductor ever asked for a ticket, we got off and then hopped on the next train. We'd pass through a couple of very small stations – just platforms in the middle of nowhere – before arriving at the Berampur station, smaller than Ginestlay's, and on the outskirts of town. But my brothers would only let me go as far as the station; I couldn't go wandering off into the town, where I might get lost. So I'd hang around the platforms while they worked, then go back home with them. Instead of food we had a lot of freedom, and we liked it.

One night, when I was five years old, I was at home, tired from a day playing out in the streets, but excited that tonight almost the whole family was gathered for dinner. My mother was home from work and, more unusually, Guddu had come back to see us. Kallu was the only one missing.

That evening, Guddu stayed for about an hour, as the four of us ate together. As Guddu was the eldest, it was he that I looked up to the most. He hadn't been home for some time and I missed hanging out with him and Kallu as a gang. I'd begun to feel I wasn't a little boy anymore, to be left at home while they were out in the world.

When our mother went out, perhaps to see if she could get us some more food, Guddu announced that he was leaving – going back to Berampur. The thought of being left behind, as always, a little kid stuck at home with nothing to do, was too much. I jumped up and said, 'I'm coming with you!' It was early evening – if I went with him, there was little likelihood of him getting me back home that night. We'd have to stay together. He thought about it for a moment and then agreed – I was thrilled. We left Shekila sitting on the floor and were gone before my mother returned. She probably wouldn't have been too worried, with me in my brother's care.

Soon, I was laughing as we sped through the night, Guddu doubling me on a bike he had hired through the quiet streets to the train station. What could be better? I'd travelled with my brothers before, but that night was different. I was going off with Guddu without a plan for when we were coming home or where we might sleep, just like he did with Kallu. I didn't know how long he would let me stay with him, but as we raced through the streets I didn't care.

I still vividly remember the ride. I sat on the bar just behind the bike's handlebars with my feet resting on either side of the front wheel axle. It was a bumpy trip, as there were potholes everywhere in the road, but I didn't mind at all. There were a lot of glowbugs flying in the air, and we passed some kids chasing them. A boy yelled out, 'Hey, Guddu!' but we rode on. I was proud that Guddu was known about town. I had even heard him being mentioned once when I was on a train – I thought he was famous. We had to keep a good lookout for people walking on the street in the dark, especially when we went under the low railway bridge. Then Guddu said we'd walk the rest of the way. Maybe he was tired with me on board too. So I hopped off and he pushed the bike along the main street to the station, past the busy chai sellers. When we were near the station entrance, Guddu hid the hire bike behind some thick bushes and we walked across the overpass to wait for the next train.

By the time the train pulled in noisily and we had scuttled aboard, I was already becoming sleepy. We got as comfortable as we could on the hard wooden seats, but the fun of the adventure was starting to wear off. I rested my head on Guddu's shoulder as the train left the station. It was getting late, and we'd be on the train for about an hour. I don't know if Guddu was having second thoughts about letting me come, but I was starting to feel a bit guilty, because my mother usually needed me to babysit Shekila while she was at work, and I didn't know when I'd be back.

By the time we got off at Berampur, I was so exhausted I slumped onto a wooden bench on the platform and said I couldn't go on without a rest. Guddu said that was fine – there were a few things he needed to do anyway. 'Just sit down and don't move. I'll come back in a little while and we can find somewhere to sleep the night.' He was probably going to scavenge some food, or hunt for coins around the platforms. I lay down, shut my eyes and must have fallen asleep straightaway.

When I woke up, it was very quiet and the station was deserted. Bleary-eyed, I looked around for Guddu but couldn't see him anywhere. There was a train at the platform where we'd got off, with its carriage door open, but I didn't know if it was the same one, or how long I'd been asleep.

I've often wondered exactly what I thought right then. I was still half-asleep and unnerved by finding myself alone at night. My thoughts were muddled. Guddu wasn't around but he'd said he wasn't going far – maybe he'd got back on the train? I shuffled over and climbed the boarding stairs to have a look. I have a memory of seeing some people asleep on board, and stepping back down in case they woke up and called a conductor. Guddu had said I should stay put, but he was probably on board in a different carriage, working, sweeping underneath the seats. What if I fell asleep on the dark platform again and the train pulled out and I was left alone?

I looked into a different carriage and found no-one, but the empty wooden bench seats were more comfortable and felt safer than the quiet station – Guddu would come and get me soon, smiling, perhaps with a treat he'd found while cleaning. There was plenty of room to stretch out. In a few moments, I was sleeping peacefully again.

This time, I must have slept properly. When I awoke, it was broad daylight and the full sun was glaring straight into my eyes. And, I realised with a jolt, the train was moving – rattling steadily along its tracks.

I jumped up. There was still no-one in my carriage, and the landscape outside the barred windows was passing quickly. My brother was nowhere to be seen. I had been left undisturbed, a small boy asleep, alone on a speeding train.

The low-class carriages weren't connected to each other with internal doors. Travellers boarded and exited their carriage from doors on the outside at each end. I raced to one end of the carriage and tried the doors on either side – they were both locked, or wouldn't budge. I ran down the other end – the doors there were locked too.

I can still feel the icy chill of panic that hit me when I realised I was trapped – a feeling of being weak, hyperactive and incredulous, all in one. I don't recall exactly what I did in that moment – screamed, banged the windows, cried, cursed. I was frantic, my heart beating triple-time. I couldn't read any of the signs in the carriage, which might have told me where I was heading or even how to get out. I ran up and down and looked beneath all the benches, in case someone else was asleep somewhere. There was only me. But I kept running up and down, yelling out my brother's name, begging him to come and get me. I called for my mother, and my brother Kallu too, but all in vain. No-one answered and the train didn't stop.

I was lost.

Slowly, I found myself shrinking from the enormity of what confronted me, hunching up into a protective ball. For a long time, I either cried or sat in a quiet daze.

After long hours hurtling along in the empty carriage, I roused myself to look out the window to see if I could recognise some landmarks. The world outside looked similar to my home, but it had no distinguishing features. I didn't know where I was headed, but I'd travelled much further than ever before. I was already far away from home.

I entered some kind of hibernating state – my system shut down, I suppose, exhausted at trying to deal with what was happening. I wept and slept, and sometimes looked out the window. There was nothing to eat, but there was water to drink from the tap in the filthy toilet cubicles at the rear, with their pit holes open to the tracks below.

Once, I woke up to realise that we'd stopped – we'd pulled in to a station. My spirits soared, as I thought I could catch someone's attention on the platform. But there wasn't a soul to be seen in the gloom. I still couldn't budge the exit doors. I beat them with my fists and screamed and screamed as the train gave a lurch and started moving again.

Eventually, I was spent. You can't remain in a state of sheer panic and terror indefinitely, and both had run their course.

Ever since, I've thought that must be why we cry: our bodies are coping with something our minds and hearts can't absorb by themselves. All that crying had served its purpose – I'd let my body work through my feelings, and now, surprisingly, I began to feel a little better. I was exhausted by the experience, and fell in and out of sleep. When I think back now and re-live the full horror of being trapped alone, with no idea where I was or where I was heading, it's like a nightmare. I remember it in snapshots – awake at the windows, terrified; curled up and drifting in and out of sleep. I think the train pulled into some stations, but the doors never opened, and somehow no-one ever saw me.

But as time passed, perhaps some of the resilience I'd built up when exploring my own town started to reassert itself. I began to think, if I can't get out by myself, then I'll just have to wait until someone lets me out, and then work out how to get home. I would behave like my brothers would behave. They were away for days at a time; I could do that too. They had shown me how to find a place to sleep, and I had looked after myself before, finding things and begging. And maybe if this train took me away from home, it could take me back home. I sat and looked out, and tried not to think about anything except the world going by the window. I would see where it all led.

*

Gradually, the countryside became greener than I'd ever seen it before. There were lush fields and tall trees with no branches but great shaggy bunches of fronds at their tops. When the sun came out from behind clouds, everything exploded into bright green light. I saw monkeys running through the tangled undergrowth by the sides of the tracks, and amazing brightly coloured birds. There was water everywhere, in rivers, lakes, ponds and fields. It was a new world to me. Even the people looked a little different.

After a while, the train began to pass through small towns, and I saw kids playing by the tracks while their mothers cooked or did the laundry on the back stoop. No-one seemed to notice a lone child at the window of the passing train. The towns got bigger and closer together, and then there were no more fields, no more open country at all, just more and more houses – streets and streets of them – roads and cars and rickshaws. There were big buildings too, and many more of them than at home, and buses and trucks, and tracks with other trains running along them, and everywhere there were people and more people, more than I had ever seen, more than I could ever have imagined living in one place.

The train eventually slowed, and I knew it must be approaching another station. Was my journey at an end this time? The train coasted until it was hardly moving at all, then gave a sudden lurch and stopped altogether. Wide-eyed, staring from behind the bars of the window, I saw crowds of people swarming on the platform, hefting luggage as they strode about. People were rushing everywhere, in their hundreds, perhaps thousands, and suddenly, someone opened one of the doors to my carriage. Without a moment's thought, I ran down the aisle as fast as I could and leapt out onto the platform. At last I was free.

Only when my parents in Hobart pointed it out on the wall map did I find out the name of the city I'd travelled to. Even if I'd been told it then, it wouldn't have meant anything to me – I'd never heard of the place. But I had arrived in what was then known as Calcutta, the sprawling megacity famous for its overpopulation, pollution and crushing poverty, one of the most intimidating and dangerous cities in the world.

I was barefoot, in a grimy pair of black shorts and a white, short-sleeved shirt with several buttons missing – truly with nothing but the clothes I was wearing. I had no money, no food and no identification of any sort. I was a little hungry, but I was used to that, so it wasn't too much of a problem yet. What I really hungered for was help.

I was thrilled to be free of my carriage prison, but frightened out of my wits by the huge station with its pressing crowds. Frantically, I looked around in the hope of seeing Guddu pushing past all the people to come and rescue me, as if he might have been stuck on the train too. But there were no familiar faces. I was paralysed, having no idea where to go or what to do, except to instinctively step out of people's way. I called out, 'Ginestlay? Berampur?' hoping that someone would tell me how to get there. But no-one in the rushing mass paid me the slightest attention.

At some point, the train I'd arrived on must have pulled away again, but I don't remember noticing. Even if I had, I doubt I would have been too keen to jump back aboard after being trapped for so long. I was scared into inaction, afraid that wandering off somewhere would make things worse. I kept to the platform, occasionally calling out, 'Berampur?'

All around me was a confusion of noise, with people shouting and calling to each other, or huddled in babbling conversation – I couldn't understand what anyone was saying. Mostly they were just very busy, pushing on and off trains in the great crush, struggling to get to wherever they needed to be as quickly as possible.

One or two people stopped to listen to me, and all I could manage to say to them was something like 'Train, Ginestlay?' Most just shook their head and walked on. One man replied, 'But "Ginestlay" is where?' I didn't know what he meant – it was just . . . *home*. How could I explain where it was? He frowned and moved on. There were a lot of children begging or hanging around the station looking for whatever they could find, just as my brothers did back home. I was just one more poor kid, crying something out, too small to make anyone stop and listen.

I steered clear of policemen, out of habit. I was afraid they might lock me up, as they'd once done to Guddu. He'd been arrested for selling toothbrush-and-paste kits at a train station, and the police had put him in jail. He'd been there for three days before we got word of his whereabouts. Conductors, police, anyone in uniform – after that, we'd avoided them all. It didn't occur to me that now they might be able to help.

I stayed on the platform even after everyone had left, having failed to get anyone's attention, sleeping on and off, unable to move away or think of what to do next. Sometime the next day, tired and miserable, I gave up trying to find help. The people in the station weren't people at all, but a great solid mass I couldn't make any impact on, like a river or the sky.

One thing I knew was that if a train had brought me to where I was, a train could take me back. The way it worked at home was that trains on the track opposite the one you arrived on went back the other way. But I'd noticed that this station was the end of the line, where all the trains came in and stopped, and then chugged back the way they had come. If no-one could tell me where the trains went, I would find out for myself.

So I boarded the next train that arrived at the platform.

Could it be as simple as that? As the train rumbled out, I got a better look at the station: it was a huge red building with many arches and towers, the biggest building I'd ever seen. I was in awe of its size, but hoped I was leaving it and its great crush of people behind forever. But after an hour or so, the train came to the end of its own line, somewhere on the outskirts of the city. Then it switched tracks and went back to the enormous station.

I caught another train and the same thing happened. Maybe the train I needed left from another platform? There were many more platforms here than at the station near home, and each seemed to have several different kinds of trains – some had lots of compartments with porters helping people on, while others had carriage after carriage filled with people on bench seats, like the one that had brought me here. The number of them was frightening, but one of them must go back to where I'd come from – I just had to keep trying.

And so that's what I did. Every day – for day after day – I caught a different train out of the city.

I hoped to avoid being locked in a carriage again by travelling only during the day. At the beginning of each trip I would watch the passing scenery hopefully, thinking yes, yes, this feels like the one that will get me home, I've seen that building or those trees before . . . Sometimes the train would reach the end of its journey and then head back again. Other times, it simply stopped at the final station on the line, and I'd be stuck in that unfamiliar, empty place until the next day, when the train began the return leg. The only times I got off a train before it reached the end of its journey was when night was falling. Then I'd crawl under the seats inside the station so that I couldn't be easily seen and curl up tight for warmth. Luckily, the weather was never very cold.

I survived by eating scraps of food I found on the ground, like peanuts travellers had dropped or corncobs not completely eaten, and fortunately it wasn't hard to find taps for a drink. This wasn't too different from the way I'd lived before, so although I was often scared and miserable, I knew how to get by, and I suppose my system was used to it. I was learning how to live on my own.

And so I shuttled back and forth, trying different platforms, travelling different routes – sometimes seeing something I recognised and realising I'd accidentally caught a train I'd tried before – and in the end not getting anywhere at all.

On all those journeys, no-one ever asked me for a ticket. Of course, I avoided trains when I could see they had conductors on them, just like we did at home, but once I was on, I was never questioned. If an official had stopped me, I might have summoned the courage to try to ask for help, but none ever did. Once, a porter appeared to understand that I was lost, but when

I couldn't immediately make myself understood he made it clear I wasn't to bother him anymore. The world of adults was closed to me, so I continued to try to solve my problem by myself.

After a while, though – perhaps even a couple of weeks – I began to lose heart. My home was out there somewhere, but maybe no train from here went there. Or maybe there was some sort of complication I couldn't work out. All I knew about the city outside of the station was what I'd seen from train windows, arriving or leaving. Maybe out there was someone who could help me, give me directions to get home, or even just give me some food.

But by now I was growing more and more familiar with the sprawling red station. It felt like my only real connection with where I'd come from, whereas the masses of people coming and going outside frightened me. Each time I went on a trip to a new and strange place, I was glad to get back to the big station, where I knew my way around and knew where to sleep or where I was most likely to find food. Of course, more than anything I still wanted to find my mother, but I was adjusting to life at the station.

I had noticed a group of children who seemed to always be at the end of a particular platform, where they'd huddle together in some old blankets at night. They seemed to be like me, with nowhere to go, but they didn't try to hide under seats or on trains. I'd watched them, and they had probably seen me, but they had shown no interest in my presence. I hadn't been confident enough to approach them, but my lack of trust was worn down by my failure to find home. Adults had proven to be of no assistance, but maybe other children would help? At least they might let me stay near them, and perhaps I'd be safer with more kids around.

The children weren't welcoming, but they didn't chase me off either as I lay on a hard wooden seat close to them and rested my head on my hands. Kids on their own were not an uncommon sight here, and one more addition to their ranks didn't surprise anyone. Exhausted from the day's train travels but a little relieved I had decided I wasn't going to start all over again the next day, I felt more secure with the others nearby and fell asleep quickly.

Before long, though, I was disturbed by what at first I thought was a bad dream. I heard young voices screaming out, 'Go away, let me go!' More shouting followed, in both young and older voices, and in the dim light from the station I thought I could make out a man yelling what I thought was something like, 'You are coming with me!' Then a child unmistakably screamed out, 'RUUUNN!' and I leapt to my feet, knowing it was no dream.

In the confusion, I saw children being lifted by adult hands and carried off, and a small girl struggling with a man by the edge of a platform. I ran for my life, sprinting away down a darkened platform and leaping off the end of it, down onto the tracks, before charging into the darkness.

Running virtually blind alongside a large wall, I kept looking over my shoulder to see if I was being chased, but didn't slow down even when I thought there was no-one behind me. I didn't know what had happened back at the station, why the men were grabbing the kids. All I knew was there was no way I was going to get caught myself.

But there was danger ahead as well as behind. As the track turned to the right, I found myself face-to-face with the blinding lights of a train coming straight towards me. I jumped to one side as it hurtled by with a deafening roar, terrifyingly close to my body. I had to press myself as hard as I could against the wall for what felt like an eternity as the train kept passing, with my face shoved sideways to keep clear of anything that might be sticking out from a carriage.

When the train had passed, I had the chance to recover. Although I was terrified at the dangers in this new city, I'd lived by my wits for long enough not to lose them now. I suppose the advantage of being five was that I didn't think too much about what had happened to the other childen, or what it meant, other than that I wanted to avoid it. What choice did I have but to keep going?

I continued to follow the tracks, but more cautiously. When they came to a road, I left them, and hence the station, for the first time on foot since I'd arrived. The road was busy, which felt safer than being somewhere out of sight, and soon led to the bank of a huge river over which stretched a massive bridge, dark against the grey sky. I remember distinctly the overwhelming impression the sight made on me. I'd seen a few bridges from the windows of trains, bigger than the only one I knew from home, which crossed the little river I played in with my brothers. In the gaps between the shop stalls huddled along the top of the riverbank, I could see the wide expanse of water, busy with boats. The bridge loomed over it, an immense structure, with people teeming along its walkway, and a slow but noisy mass of bicycles, motorbikes, cars and trucks on its road. It was an astonishing sight for a little boy from a small village. How many people were here? Was this the biggest place in the world? The opening up of the city beyond the station made me feel more lost than ever.

I stayed on the street for some time, stunned by the scale of the scene, but while I seemed invisible, I worried that I could come to the attention of people like the men I'd just escaped – or even the very same men, who might be chasing me. Those thoughts gave me the courage to walk past the shop stalls and between some larger buildings, towards the riverbank. The steep grassy slopes, shaded by big leafy trees, quickly gave way to the muddy river's edge, and the whole area was full of activity – there were people bathing as others nearby washed cooking pots and bowls in the shallows, some tending small open fires, and porters ferried all manner of things up the banks from long, low boats.

Back at home, I had been a very curious child – once I'd become old enough to be allowed away from the house on my own, I'd never liked to stay in one place much. I was always keen to see what was around the next corner, which is why I'd been so eager to start living the life of my brothers, on the move and independent, and why I'd quickly chosen to leave the house with Guddu that night. But being lost in the big train station in this unsettlingly huge city had stifled that instinct – I ached for the familiar streets of home. It had made me think better of straying too far from the small area I already knew. I was torn between going back to the station and the close, confusing streets, and the more open but unfamiliar territory of the riverbank. There was more and more of this city as far as I could see in every direction. Exhausted from the day's trials and lack of proper food and sleep, I kept out of people's way, but had no idea what to do next. I tried hanging around some of the food stalls, to see if anyone might give me something to eat, but they shooed me away.

Eventually, I walked along the riverbank a little and came upon a group of sleeping people that I recognised as holy men. I'd seen men like these back at home. They were not like Baba, at his mosque back home: Baba wore a long white shirt and pants, like many men in my neighbourhood. These men were barefoot and wore saffron robes and beads, and some of them were quite scary looking, with wild clumps of dirty long hair wound on their heads and red and white paint on their faces. They were grubby, like me, from living outdoors on the streets. I had been keeping away from adults as best I could, but surely no-one bad would find me here, among holy people? I lay down near the men, curled up into a ball, and joined my hands to pillow my head.

Before I knew it, morning had come and I was alone. The holy men had left, but the sun was up and there were people walking about. I had survived my first night on the streets of Calcutta.

3

SURVIVAL

Hungry, as usual, I found that at least there were more possibilities for food along the wide river than inside the big red train station to which I'd been transported days earlier.

As the stallholders had seemed indifferent to begging children, I went along the water's edge, thinking I might find people cooking there. Daylight confirmed that this was the biggest river I'd ever seen, but it was also fouler and smellier, lined with dead animals, human excrement and filth. As I picked my way along its edge, I was horrified to see two dead people lying among the piles of rubbish, one with his throat cut, the other with his ears chopped off. I'd seen dead bodies before, when people had died at home and others saw that they were treated respectfully. But I hadn't come across any just lying outside. Here, no-one seemed to pay any more attention to dead people than to dead animals, even if they seemed to have been violently attacked. These bodies lay in the open, under a hot sun, covered with flies and – it appeared – gnawed by rats.

The sight made me feel sick, but what struck me most powerfully was that it confirmed what I'd already begun to feel – that every day in this city was a matter of life and death. There was danger everywhere, and in everyone – there were robbers and people who took children and even killers. It opened up all sorts of fears. Was this the world that my brothers lived in when they went away, and the reason they never let me leave the stations when I travelled with them? What had happened to Guddu at the train station? Where had he got to and why hadn't he been there when I woke up? Was he somewhere like this, looking for me? And what did my family think had happened to me? Were they looking, or did they think I was dead, gone, lost forever?

More than anything I wanted to get to my mother, to Guddu, to our family, to be protected and cared for, but I also knew that to have any hope of that I would have to be as strong as I could be. Otherwise, I would disappear, or even die, here on the bank of the wide, murky river. I understood that I had to rely on myself. I pulled myself together.

I turned back towards the bridge and came to some stone steps leading into the river, with people bathing and doing laundry on them. There was a wide stone drain next to the steps, which brought water and waste down into the river from the street. Kids were playing, splashing and fooling about in the water, so I went over to join in. Now it strikes me – just as it strikes many visitors to India – as incredible that anyone would wash or bathe in a river that was also a sewer and mortuary, but at the time I didn't give it a second thought. It was a river – rivers were for all of those things. They were also sites of extraordinary acts of kindness, as I was to discover.

The other children seemed to accept me joining in and we played about in the water, a respite from the heat of the day. While some were very confident, leaping off the side of the steps out into the river, I only walked down them far enough to be up to my knees – although my brothers had tried to teach me to swim in the dammed river near our town, I hadn't caught on yet. At home, other than in the monsoon, the river was just a gentle stream to splash in. But I loved being in the water. And never more than on this day – it felt wonderful to simply be a child again, playing with other kids.

Later in the afternoon, the other children went home. I stayed on the steps, not wanting the day to end. But the river was full of surprises. I hadn't noticed, but the water level must have been rising through the day, and when I jumped in to what had been a safe spot earlier on, I suddenly found myself in much deeper water – over my head. There was a strong current too, which was carrying me further from the steps. Splashing and flailing desperately, I pushed off from the river bottom and struggled back to the surface to gasp a breath of air, but the water dragged me down and out again. This time I was too far out to reach the bottom. I was drowning.

Then I heard a splash nearby and found myself wrenched upwards, pulled to the surface and onto the steps, where I sat spluttering and coughing up murky water. I had been saved by a homeless old man who had jumped in off the stone drain to reach me just in time and pluck me from the water. Then he silently made his way back up the steps and onto the riverbank, where I suppose he lived.

Perhaps the kindness of that stranger lowered my guard, or perhaps I was just a five-year-old, but when I went back to swim in the river the next day, stupidly I let the rising tide and strong current surprise me again, and once more got into trouble. Amazingly, the same man rescued me – perhaps he'd kept an eye out when he saw me come back. This time, other people noticed what had happened, seeing the man helping me up onto the steps, where I hacked up more water. A crowd formed around us, and I understood enough to realise they were declaring that the gods had spared me, that it had not yet been my time to die.

Maybe I felt overwhelmed by all the people pushing up close to stare at me, or just humiliated or annoyed with myself for having almost drowned a second time, but I leapt to my feet and ran away, as fast as I could. I went far along the bank, until I couldn't run anymore, vowing to keep out of the river.

So I don't think I ever thanked the homeless man, almost my guardian angel, for rescuing me, not once but twice.

To escape the crowd, I had run away from the area I had come to know, and night was falling. It was too late to try to get back to my part of the riverbank before dark, so I had to quickly find somewhere nearby to sleep. I came upon what looked like a disused factory, with a large pile of rubbish in the shadows at the back. Exhausted, I found a piece of cardboard and lay down on it behind the rubbish heap. The place had a bad smell, but I was becoming used to that by now, and at least it was out of sight.

That night, I was woken by a pack of scary-looking dogs barking under a nearby streetlight. I kept a rock in my hand, and a pile of others within easy reach, and must have fallen asleep like that, because when I woke with the hot sun full in my face, the rocks were still there but the dogs were nowhere to be seen.

Over the next little while, I came to know the neighbourhood around the station, including the little shops and stalls where

I foraged for food. The smells coming from those shops were irresistible: mangoes and watermelons, fried savouries, and gulab jamuns and laddus from the sweets stalls. And then all I could see was people eating: a group of men cracking peanuts and chatting, some others having chai and sharing a small bunch of grapes. Hunger gnawed at me then, and I would go to every shopkeeper and beg. They always chased me away, along with the half-dozen or so other children hanging around – there were too many of us to take pity on.

I'd watch people eating – they were poor people like my family, so they didn't usually leave good food behind, but they might drop something or not finish it entirely. There were no bins, so when a person was done with something, they simply threw it on the ground. I worked out what leftovers could be safely eaten, just as back at home my brothers and I knew which food to scavenge on a railway platform. Bits of fried food, like a samosa, were pretty safe once you scraped off the dirt, but they were highly prized. The race would be on to snatch up the remains before the other scavenging kids. Mostly I relied on things easily spilled, like nuts or spicy bhuja mix, with dried chick peas and lentils. Sometimes I'd race for a bit of flat bread. There were struggles between those equally desperate for scraps, and sometimes I found myself roughly shoved aside or even punched. We were like wild dogs fighting over a bone.

Although I stayed mostly near the station and the river to sleep, I began to explore a few of the surrounding streets. It might have been a return of natural wandering inclinations, but my explorations were also driven by the hope that around that next corner might be something to eat, some source of food that the other street kids hadn't found – a kindly stallholder or box of rejects from the market. A place this big was full of possibilities.

It was also full of dangers. On one expedition, I remember finding myself in a dense couple of blocks of tumbledown houses and shacks put together with bamboo and rusty corrugated iron. The smell was truly awful, as if something had died. I became aware of people looking at me strangely, as if I had no right to be around there, and encountered a group of older boys smoking leaf-wrapped cigarettes. I was starting to feel unnerved and stopped in my tracks as they looked at me.

One boy, waving his cigarette around in his hand, stood up and approached, talking loudly at me. His friends laughed along. I couldn't understand a word and stood there, wondering what to do. Then he strode straight up and slapped my face, twice, while he kept on talking at me. Dumbfounded, I started to cry, and he hit me again, hard, and I dropped to the ground and cried while the boys laughed.

I realised things could become worse and that I had to get out of there, so I tried to collect myself. I stood up, turned around and started walking away at a steady pace, as you might do from a dangerous dog, my face stinging. Maybe if I showed I didn't want to stay in their place, they would leave me alone. But when they began to come after me, I broke into a run. Through the tears in my eyes I made out a narrow gap between two buildings and darted towards it, just as I felt a rock that one of them had thrown sting my arm.

I wriggled through the gap and emerged into an enclosed yard. I couldn't see any way out, and the boys were shouting on the other side. The ground was a sea of garbage, which washed high up the far wall – perhaps I could climb up it and get out that way. As I picked my way across the yard, the gang appeared through another entrance I hadn't seen. They started picking things out of a rusty bin, and their leader shouted at me. Then the first bottle sailed through the air and smashed against the wall behind me. More bottles followed, exploding around me – it was only a matter of time until someone got their aim right and hit me. Stumbling and ducking, I reached the rubbish heap and mercifully it held my weight. I climbed all the way up, hauled myself on top of the wall and ran along it, praying the boys wouldn't follow me. Bottles kept smashing on the wall below, and whizzing past my legs.

Maybe seeing me run was sport enough for the gang. They'd

chased me off their territory and didn't bother to follow me as I wobbled along as fast as I could. A little further on I found a bamboo ladder leaning against the wall in someone's back yard. I climbed down it and charged through the house and out the front door, past a women sitting with her baby. She didn't seem to notice me run by, as I headed as fast as I could back towards the bridge, looming in the distance.

Even on the river, as well as searching for food I was always on the lookout for a safe place to rest. Often, when I returned to somewhere I'd slept before, there'd be others already there, so I'd move on. Other times, I'd just come across a better prospect. Sleeping rough, and the constant stress of being on the lookout, meant I was always tired. Picking along the riverbank one twilight, I found myself heading under the bridge's huge structure for the first time. Beneath it, I came across a few small wooden platforms gathered together, with offerings like coconut pieces and coins, along with pictures and little statues of a goddess I recognised – Durga, the warrior form of the supreme goddess, Mahadevi. She was seated on a tiger, with her many arms whirling weapons, which in the stories I'd been told she had used to slay a demon. She was a fierce vision to behold, lit by flickering terracotta lamps. But there was also something comforting about the little lights winking in the gathering darkness all around me, and I sat there under the bridge, looking out over the river. Ever hungry, I found the offerings too tempting – I collected some of the bits of fruit and coconut and ate them. I also took some coins.

I didn't want to leave this place. I felt I would be all right here. Along with the shrines, there were some planks set as a platform to hang out over the water. I checked that its boards were stout and stable, and clambered onto it. It felt as if I was in a sacred place, where people came to pray to the goddess. On the hard wooden planks, listening to the sound of the river flowing by beneath me, I thought about my family, wondering how they were and how they must be thinking the same thing about me.

But as I recall it, the feelings I had were now different from when I'd first arrived – less sharp, less painful, but somehow deeper too. Even if home was the same, I was different. I still wanted to get back there, desperately, but the feeling didn't completely swamp me. I hadn't given up hope of returning to my family, but I had become more focused on surviving here, on getting through the days. I suppose I was more aware of living here than of living at a home I couldn't find. That home – the home I'd lost – felt even further away. Maybe I had come to feel to some degree that *this* was my home now, at least for the time being.

When I woke up the next morning, one of the wild-looking holy men in saffron robes was meditating nearby. Soon others arrived and joined him, some stripped to the waist and some carrying long decorated walking sticks. I left quietly. I knew that I had slept in their place and taken some of their offerings, and that maybe they intended the boards over the water to be another little shrine to Durga. But they hadn't harmed me, or even woken me, and in that moment I felt secure in their company, almost as if we were on our journeys side-by-side.

Some days, with little else to do, I would go back to the rail yards and wander among the many lines of track. There were always others about, looking for whatever they could find or else just filling up their days, like I was. Maybe they were lost too, wondering which track might lead them home. Occasionally, a train would go by, sounding its horn to warn people out of its way.

One quiet but very hot day, I walked around until I was dazed from heat, then sat down on a track, almost falling asleep. A man dressed in a grimy white shirt and trousers came over and asked something about what I was doing hanging around such a dangerous place. When I replied in my halting way, he not only understood me, but replied more slowly and carefully, so I could understand him. He said that many children were hit by trains and killed here, and others lost arms and legs. Train stations and railway yards were dangerous places, he said, not playgrounds for children.

I told him that I was lost, and, encouraged by the fact that he seemed to be patient enough to listen and work out what I was saying, I explained that I came from Ginestlay, but no-one seemed to know where that was, and now I was alone with no family and no place to live. After listening to my story – the first time I'd been able to properly tell it to anyone – he told me he would take me to his home and give me food and water and a place to sleep. I was overjoyed. Somebody had at last stopped to help and was going to save me. I didn't hesitate to go with him.

He was a railway worker and lived in a little shack by the side of the tracks, near the point at which they all converged at the entrance to the immense red station. The shack was made of corrugated iron sheets patched with some panels of thick cardboard, and was kept up by a wooden frame. He shared it with a group of other railway workers, and I was invited to join them all for dinner. For the first time since I had become lost, I sat at a table and ate a meal that someone had cooked and that was still warm – I still remember it being a lentil daal with rice that one of the workers made over a little fire in a corner of the shack. The workers didn't seem to mind that I was there, and didn't complain about having to share their dinner. They were very poor, but they had just enough to live by different laws from people on the streets. They had a roof, and enough for a plain meal, and a job, however hard it was. They could only offer me a tiny amount, but it made all the difference because of their willingness to feed and house a stranger. It was like crossing into an entirely different world from the one I'd been living in, and all it took to make it was a few sheets of corrugated iron and a handful of lentils. For the second time, it felt like the kindness of a stranger had saved my life.

There was a simple spare bed in the back of the shack, made out of straw, and I slept there almost as comfortably and happily as if I was already back at home. The railway worker had mentioned that he knew someone who might be able to help me, and the next day he said that he had arranged for this man to visit. I was overwhelmed with relief – already it seemed like the whole experience was a bad dream. Soon I would be home. I spent the day in the shack after the men headed off to work, waiting for my saviour.

As promised, the next day another man turned up, and he also spoke carefully in plain terms I understood. He was well dressed in a neat suit and he laughed when I pointed at his distinctive moustache and said, 'Kapil Dev,' referring to India's cricket captain at the time, whom he looked like. He sat down on my bed and said, 'Come over here and tell me where you are from.' So I did as he asked, and told him what had happened to me. He wanted to know as much as possible about where I was from, so that he could help me find the place, and as I tried my best to explain everything, he lay down on the bed and had me lie down beside him.

Many lucky and unlucky things happened to me on my journey, and I made good and bad decisions. My instincts weren't always sound, but they had been sharpened by weeks of living on the streets, making conscious and unconscious decisions about risk. If you survive, you learn to trust your instincts. Perhaps any five-year-old would have begun to feel uneasy, lying beside a strange man on a bed. Nothing untoward happened, and the man didn't lay a hand on me, but despite the marvellous, intoxicating promises I was being made about finding my home, I knew something wasn't right. I also knew that I shouldn't show him that I didn't trust him, that I should play along. While he was saying that the next day we would go together to a place he knew and try to get me back home, I nodded and agreed. At the same time, I knew beyond question that I should have nothing to do with this man, and that I had to make a plan to get away.

That night after dinner, I washed the dishes in a worn old tub in the corner near the door, as I'd done the previous two nights. The men went into their usual huddle for their chai and a smoke, and were soon completely distracted by their conversation and jokes. This was my chance. I picked the best moment I could and bolted out the door. I ran as if my life depended on it, which in retrospect I fear it did. I hoped that by taking them by surprise, I'd get enough of a headstart to escape pursuit. Once more, I was fleeing into the night past the railway tracks and down streets I did not know, with no idea where to go, no thought but escape.

I was quickly exhausted and slowed down once I was in crowded streets – maybe they wouldn't even care that I was gone, and even if they did, surely they couldn't have followed me this far. Then I heard someone call out my name from quite close behind. That sent a jolt through my body like an electric shock. Immediately, I ducked down, although I was already much shorter than the people all around me, and headed for the most crowded parts of the narrow street, near the bustling stalls hawking food along the curb. When I looked around, I could glimpse a couple of men who looked like they might be follow-ing me – grim, hard-faced men, looking around and moving fast. Then I realised one of them was the railway worker I'd first met, who no longer looked much like the kind man who'd taken me in. I hurried away from them, but the street soon became so crowded it was hard to move fast, and I felt that the men were getting closer. I had to hide. I found a small gap between two houses and ducked into it, crawling back as far as I could, before I came to a leaking sewerage pipe in one of the walls large enough for me to hide in. I backed into it on all fours until I couldn't be seen from the street, ignoring the cobwebs, and the foul-smelling water running over my hands. I was much more scared of what was out there than I was of the dark pipe. If they found me there was no way out.

I heard one of them talking to the fruit-juice seller whose stand was right next to where I was hidden. I even have a frightening memory of peering out just as the railway worker himself looked into the gap towards the pipe, searching with hard eyes that seemed for a moment to stop on me, and after a hesitation, moved on. Did I really come that close to being discovered? Was it the man who had taken me in that I saw? I can't be sure now, but the scene has remained with me as such a vivid image perhaps due to the power of the betrayal – I had trusted this man and believed that he was going to help me, only for the ground to open up beneath me and try to swallow me up. I've never forgotten that terrifying feeling.

I stayed hidden for some time, until I was certain he and the others had left, then slipped out and made my way through the darkest of the alleys and streets. I was heartbroken that all my hopes had come to nothing, but also extremely relieved to have escaped. At least my survival instincts seemed to be strong. At some level, I took strength from being able to look after myself.

4

SALVATION

I was so scared of being found again by the railway worker and the other men that I didn't dare remain near the railway station. Despite my occasional forays into the nearby neighbourhood, until then I had still been too cautious to travel far from the point at which I had first arrived in the city. But now I had to. I decided to cross the river for the first time.

The walkways on either side of the long bridge were as crowded as the platforms at the station, but with many more different types of people. Most were hurrying to and fro, by themselves or in groups, looking very busy, but some were just hanging around as though they lived there, above the water. I had to dodge families shuffling along in knots and people ferrying enormous piles of goods on their heads. I passed beggars missing limbs and eyes, some with faces ravaged and eaten away by disease, all calling up with their metal begging bowls for a rupee or some food. The road in the middle was crawling with traffic of all kinds, including rickshaws and bullock carts, and even stray cows wandering through the fray. The scale of it all overwhelmed me. I pushed through as best I could, and got off the main road as soon as I was on the other side.

Now in quieter surroundings, I wandered a maze of alleys and streets aimlessly, keeping watch for both trouble and help. The railway worker had made it harder to tell the difference. Although being tricked had given me some faith in my street-smarts, maybe it had also taught me that I couldn't survive on my own for very long – the dangers were too great and too hard to see. My suspicion of people had been reinforced – they were either indifferent or bad – but so had my need to find that rare person who could genuinely help me, like the homeless man by the river. I wanted to stay away from people but also find a way out of where I was. That meant I needed to keep extremely alert. The combination of wariness and the need to take a chance characterised the rest of my journey.

I began to approach people a little more. At some point, walking along one of the streets of my new neighbourhood, I came across a boy about the same age as me, talking aloud to himself, or to the world at large. When he saw me watching him, he said hello and we talked shyly for a bit. He seemed to know more words than me, to speak more like an adult, so he probably went to school, but he was friendly and we played around on the street for a while. Then he said I could go with him to his house. Cautiously, I followed.

When we got there, he introduced me to his mother, and I told them a little of what had happened to me. The mother told me that I could share a meal with them, and maybe stay with them until they could find someone who might be able to get me home. My wariness slipped away in the face of what seemed genuine concern. I couldn't imagine the friendly woman meaning me any harm, and here was a chance to get off the streets. Even that short time in the railway worker's house had broken the habits of sleeping rough – now I wanted the safety of being inside more, not less. I felt very happy that I was in a home, fed and sheltered.

The next day the mother said I could go out with her and her son, and we walked to a pond nearby, where the locals did their laundry. She set about washing their clothes there, and the boy and I washed ourselves too. I had worn the same black shorts and short-sleeved white shirt since I'd become lost, and I must have been very dirty. I loved being in water where I didn't need to be able to swim, and as usual could have stayed there forever. But the day wore on, and my new friend got out and was dried and dressed when his mother started to call for me to join them. Perhaps having forgotten the ways of families and the respect expected for a mother's authority, I kept splashing about, not wanting to leave. The mother quickly lost her temper and flung a rock that missed me by a whisker. I started crying; the mother took her son, turned and left.

I don't remember exactly what I felt, standing there in the shallows of the pond. Maybe I had misunderstood? Maybe by staying in the water I had made them think I didn't want to join them? My mother would never have thrown a rock at me, even if she thought I was misbehaving. But the ease with which the woman had turned her back on me was the same as the ease with which she had welcomed me into her house. Was this just how people were in the big city?

Although they had left me on my own again, meeting them had still been a positive experience: as well as being given another proper meal and a place indoors to sleep, I had discovered that there were perhaps more people than I'd first thought who could be made to understand what I was saying. And, not long afterwards, I found another.

One day I was hanging around near a shopfront in my new neighbourhood, seeing if there was a chance to scavenge some food, when a boy about the age of my brother Guddu came along, carrying goods on a handcart. I have no idea what made him notice me, but he said something to me I didn't understand. He wasn't aggressive at all, so I didn't panic; I just stood and looked at him as he walked over. Then he spoke more deliberately, asking me what I was doing and what was my name.

We talked for a bit and I admitted I was lost, and he invited me to stay with his family. I might have hesitated, wondering whether he meant me harm or would turn on me, as the little boy's mother had, but I went with him. It was a risk, but so was staying on the streets. And that subconscious calculator of risk, instinct, told me this boy meant well.

My instincts were right. He was very friendly, and I stayed at his family home for several days. Sometimes I went out with him and helped with his work hefting goods on and off his cart, and he was patient and seemed to be looking out for me. And I soon learned that he was doing much more for me than that.

One day he began talking with me in what seemed like a different way, more adult, more serious. He told me he was taking me to a place where I might be able to get help, and we went across town together. He took me to a large police station, with many officers. Immediately, I began to resist. Was this a trick? Was he having me arrested? The teenager calmed me down, promising that the policemen didn't mean any harm, that they would try to find my home and family. I didn't really understand what was going on, but went inside with him. The teenager spoke to the police for some time, and eventually came back to me to say that he was going to leave me in their care. I didn't want him to go, and I was still very nervous about the police, but my trust in this boy was strong enough to allow me to stay. I didn't know what else I could do. I was sad and scared when he said goodbye, but he said he'd done all he could, and that this was the best way for me to find my way home. I hope that I thanked him.

Soon after the teenager left, I was taken out the back of the station to the lockup, where I was put in a cell and the door locked. I had no idea if things were taking a turn for the better or worse. I didn't know it then, but in fact, as literally as the homeless man by the river, the teenager had saved my life.

Sometimes I wonder what would have happened to me had he not taken me in, or had I refused to trust him. It's possible someone else would have done the same thing he did, eventually, or that I would have been collected by some organisation for homeless kids. But it's more likely I would have died on the street. Today, there are perhaps a hundred thousand homeless kids in Kolkata, and a good many of them die before they reach adulthood.

Of course, I can't be sure what the railway worker's friend planned, or what happened to the children who were grabbed from the station that night I slept nearby, but I feel pretty sure that they faced greater horrors than I ever did. No-one knows how many Indian children have been trafficked into the sex trade, or slavery, or even for organs, but all these trades are thriving, with too few officials and too many kids.

It was only a couple of years after my period on the streets that the notorious 'Stoneman' murders began in Calcutta, following the same phenomenon in Bombay. Somebody started murdering homeless people bedding down at night, especially around the city's major station, by dropping a large rock or slab of concrete onto their heads as they slept. Thirteen people died over a six-month period and no-one was ever charged (though the killings stopped after the police detained a psychologically disturbed suspect). Had I stayed on the street, there's every chance I wouldn't be alive today, and certainly not writing this book.

Despite having so many memories that I wish I could forget, one thing I have always wished I could remember was that teenager's name.

I slept that night in the police lockup. The next morning, some policemen came and reassured me that I wasn't under arrest or in trouble, and that they were going to try to help. I didn't feel at all comfortable with the situation, but I went along with what they said. It was my first step on the journey that took me half-way around the world.

I was given food, then put into a big paddy wagon with other children, both older and younger than me. We were driven through town to a building where some official-looking people gave us lunch and a drink. They asked me lots of questions, and although I didn't always understand them, it was clear that they wanted to know who I was and where I had come from. I told them what I could. They recorded my answers on their many forms and documents. 'Ginestlay' meant nothing to them. I struggled to remember the name of the place I'd boarded the train but could only say my brothers called it something like 'Burampour', 'Birampur', 'Berampur . . .'

Although they took notes, they didn't really have a hope of finding these half-remembered names of comparatively tiny places that could be anywhere in the country. I didn't even know my full name. I was just 'Saroo'. In the end, without knowing who I was or where I'd come from, they declared my status as 'Lost'.

After they finished their questioning, I was taken in another van to another building, a home that they said was for children like me, who had nowhere else to go. We pulled up outside a massive rusted iron door, like a prison gate, with a tiny doorway in the wall next to it. I wondered whether, if I went in there,

I ever would come out. But I'd come this far. I didn't want to go back to the streets.

Inside, there was a compound of large buildings called 'the home'. The one I was taken to was immense – two storeys with hundreds, maybe thousands, of children playing or sitting in groups. I was taken into a huge hall with rows and rows of bunk beds stretching its length. Way down the end of the hall, there was a communal bathroom.

I was shown to a bunk bed with a mosquito net, which I would be sharing with a little girl, and given food and drink. At first the home seemed how I had imagined school to be, but this school had rooms with beds, and you lived there, a little more like a hospital, or even a prison. Certainly, over time it felt more like a prison than a school, but initially I was happy to be there, sheltered and fed.

I soon learned that there was a second hall above mine with just as many bunks, also filled with kids. Often we slept three or four to a bed, and were sometimes moved around so we ended up sharing with different people, or sleeping on the floor if there were too many kids in the home. The bathrooms weren't cleaned often. The whole place was eerie, especially at night, when it was all too easy to imagine ghosts hiding in every corner.

I wonder now whether the feel of the place was somehow

connected with what many of the children had been through. Some had been abandoned by their families, and others had been hurt by them and taken away. I started to feel like I was one of the luckier ones. I was malnourished but not sickly, whereas I saw children with no legs or no arms, and some with no limbs at all. There were others with awful injuries and some who could not, or would not, speak. I'd seen people with abnormalities before, and disturbed people yelling out to no-one or acting crazily, especially on the streets around the station. But I could always avoid them if something about them scared me. In the home, I couldn't get away – I was living with kids with all manner of problems, including criminal and violent children who were too young to be jailed. Some were almost adults.

I later learned that this was a juvenile detention centre, called Liluah, housing problem children of any and all kinds, including lost children, but also the mentally ill and thieves, murderers and gang members. But back then I just knew it as a distressing place, where I would wake in the night to someone screaming, or lots of frightened kids crying. What would become of me here? How long was I going to live in this horrible place?

Again, I had to learn how to survive. Just as I had been picked on by boys outside, from the outset I was picked on by older boys in the home. Not having much vocabulary made me vulnerable, and being small and relatively defenceless brought out the bully and the brute in them. Bigger boys would start taunting and making fun of me, and then push me, and if I didn't manage to get away, I was bashed. I quickly learned to stay away from certain areas when it was playtime. The staff didn't seem willing to intervene, but when they did, punishment would be meted out without regard for who was to blame: a long, thin cane was fetched, which hurt doubly, because a split end pinched the skin on contact.

There were other dangers, too, which I avoided more by luck than by anything I planned. Liluah was surrounded by high walls, but I have memories of seeing people climb over them from the outside and enter the buildings. I never saw or heard what they did, but kids ran out crying before the strangers escaped. I don't know if the staff didn't care or were power-less to protect us, but it was a large place and I guess it was well known as a children's home. The types of people who tried to capture me when I was on the streets clearly didn't let walls and gates stop them. It's another thing that could have happened to me that I've tried not to think too hard about, but it's difficult not to feel upset for those who weren't so lucky. That feeling has increased as I've become older, maybe as I've learned more about the world and more about my own great good fortune. I know now that few are taken off the streets, and many of those who are have a lot of suffering ahead of them.

In the few weeks I was at the Liluah home, some kids left through the little door in the wall, but I was never really sure why they were allowed to go or where they would be going. Maybe someone had found their families? I wondered what happened to the older ones who grew into adults within the walls. Perhaps they were sent to a different place, or just released onto the streets at a certain age.

I prayed that, for whatever reason, I would be one of those who got to leave before that.

And eventually I was. Although I didn't know the reason at the time, about a month after my arrival, because no-one had reported me missing and they didn't know where I was from, the authorities decided to hand me over to an orphanage. All I knew was that I was called into the main office and told I was being sent to another home, a much nicer one. I was sent off to shower and was provided with new clothes. As always, I did as I was told. They said I was very lucky. And, although they didn't seem to have found my family, I did indeed feel very lucky to be leaving what I'd come to think of as a hellish place.

Mrs Sood, of the Indian Society for Sponsorship and Adoption (ISSA), was to become a major figure in my life.

Mrs Sood explained that the authorities had no idea who

I was or where my home and family were. She said she was going to try to find them, in places that might be the 'Berampur' I had told them about. In the meantime, I would get to live in her orphanage, called Nava Jeevan.

Nava Jeevan – which I've since learned is Hindi for 'new life' – did turn out to be much nicer than the Liluah juvenile home, and was populated mostly by little children like me. It was a blue three-storey concrete building which was far more welcoming. As we walked in, I saw a few other kids inside peering around a corner to see the new arrival – they smiled and ran off when the woman who greeted Mrs Sood and me shooed them away. I could see into a few rooms as we walked by, where the sun streamed in on the bunk beds, which were fewer in number than those in the long halls at the home. The windows had bars, but I was beginning to understand that these were for keeping us safe rather than imprisoned. The presence of colourful posters on the walls also made it seem a much friendlier environment than where I'd come from.

Although there were fewer children living here than in the home, it was still sometimes overcrowded at night, forcing some kids to sleep on the floor. That meant you might wake up damp from someone else's pee. In the mornings, we had a quick wash with water pumped from a well near the building's entrance and brush our teeth using our fingers as a toothbrush.

We were given a glass of hot milk with sweet Indian bread or a few milk biscuits.

It was usually quiet during the day, when many of the others went off to school. Because I had never been, I was left behind, sometimes alone. I spent a lot of time hanging around on the front porch, which was enclosed with bars, like a cage. I liked its view of a large pond across the street. After a while, I got to know a girl about Guddu's age who lived on the other side of the pond, and she sometimes came to visit. Occasionally, she'd pass me a snack between the bars, and one day she gave me a necklace with a pendant of the elephant-headed god, Ganesh. I was astonished. It was the first present I'd ever received from anyone. I kept the necklace hidden from the others, occasionally taking it out to gaze at in wonder. I later learnt that Ganesh is often called the Remover of Obstacles, and Lord of Beginnings. I wonder whether that was why the girl chose to give it to me. (Ganesh is also Patron of Letters, and so, in a way, is the patron of this book.)

The necklace was more than just a beautiful object to call my own; for me, it was a concrete demonstration that there were good people in the world who were trying to help me. I still have it and it's one of my most treasured possessions.

Like there had been at the home, there were bullies at the orphanage, although they were closer to my own age and I was able to keep clear of them. I generally stayed out of trouble, but one time a girl decided to run away and took me with her. I'd never thought to try to get away, but she swept me up in her plan, and we'd fled out through the doors together one morning before I knew what was happening. We got as far as a sweets stall a little way down the street, where the vendor gave us each a treat to slow us down while he alerted the Nava Jeevan staff to our whereabouts. I don't remember being punished in any way. In fact, no-one was ever smacked at the orphanage, let alone caned, though you might get a dressing-down or be made to sit alone for a spell for misbehaving.

It wasn't long before Mrs Sood told me that, despite their efforts, they hadn't managed to find my home or my family and there was nothing more they could do. Mrs Sood seemed very friendly, and I believed she was trying to help, but she said they hadn't found my mother in Berampur. She said they were going to try to find another family for me to live with. As I struggled to make sense of what she was saying, I began to see the hard truth: she was telling me I would never be going home.

A part of me had already accepted this. That initial disbelieving desperation to get home – that feeling that, unless the world was immediately put back the way it had been, I couldn't survive, couldn't exist – had long faded. The world was now what I saw around me, the situation I was in. Perhaps I had learned some of the lessons my brothers had learned when they started living on their wits away from home, although I was younger and didn't have the safety net of our mother being at hand. I'd concentrated on what I needed to do to survive, and that involved what was in front of me, not far away. Although I wondered why the adults couldn't just find the right train to take me back where I came from, and was sad at Mrs Sood's news, I don't remember being devastated by it, despite its finality.

Mrs Sood told me that families from other countries were happy to have lost Indian children live with them, and she thought she could find a new family for me, if I wanted that. I'm not sure I really understood the proposition, and I didn't give it too much thought.

But after only four weeks in Nava Jeevan, I was taken to the ISSA office, where Mrs Sood told me a mother and father had been found who wanted to take me into their home. They lived in another country – Australia. She said that it was a country India played at cricket, and I was aware of having heard that before, but I knew no more about Australia than that. Mrs Sood said that two boys I knew who had recently left – Abdul and Musa – had gone there, and that a friend I had made – Asra – had also been chosen to go there. Australia was a good place that was helping poor children without families and giving them opportunities most children in India would never have.

Back at Nava Jeevan, Asra and I were each shown bewitching little red photograph albums that the people offering to become our new families had made. Inside were pictures of them, their houses and other aspects of their lives – I looked through mine with my eyes popping out of my head. The people looked so different from what I was used to – they were white! And everything around them looked shiny, clean and new. Some of the things I'd never seen before, and the staff explained to Asra and me what they were, reading us the English captions. In my book it said: 'This is your father washing our car, in which we will visit many places.' They had a car! 'This is the house that will be our home.' It was very grand, with lots of glass windows, and it looked brand new. The book was even addressed to me: 'Dear Saroo.' The family, I was told, were called Mr and Mrs Brierley.

There was also a picture of a jet plane ('This plane will bring you to Australia'), which fascinated me. Back at home, I had seen jets flying high up in the sky, leaving their vapour trails streaking behind them, and had always wondered what it would be like to sit in a plane up in the clouds. If I agreed to go to these people, I would find out.

It was an overwhelming experience. Asra was very excited and often asked for us to be shown our books, which were held by the staff for safekeeping. She would sit down with me and open hers, point to a picture and say, 'This is my new mum' or 'This is my new house.' I would join in, 'This is *my* new house! This is *my* new dad's car!' We encouraged each other, and her enthusiasm rubbed off on me. It was a little like having a storybook all about me, even though I wasn't in it. It was hard to believe it was real. All I knew about Australia was in that red book, but I really couldn't have thought of anything else to ask.

At Nava Jeevan, everyone cried from time to time about the parents they had lost. Some children's parents had abandoned them, and some had died. I just didn't know where my family was, and no-one could help me find them. But we had all lost our families and there was no going back. Now I was being offered a chance to join a new family. Asra was already talking about hers with enthusiasm.

I don't know that I was truly given a choice, and I'm sure some gentle persuasion would have been brought to bear had I expressed doubts. But it wasn't necessary. I knew there wasn't much I could do if I didn't accept the opportunity. Go back to the home where I was bullied? Go back to the streets and keep taking my chances? Keep searching for a train not even the adults could find?

I told them I wanted to go.

My agreeing to join the new family made everyone so happy that the mood was infectious: immediately, any last reservations melted away. I was told that I'd be going to Australia very soon, to meet my new parents, and on a jet plane just like the one in the picture.

Asra and I were about the same age, but the others going to Australia were only toddlers or babies. I don't know if that made what was happening more or less scary for the littler ones – how much did they understand?

One day, we were washed and dressed nicely, and some of the boys and girls were taken in separate taxis. The boys went to the house of a woman we were told to call Aunty Ula. She was a white woman from Sweden, although of course that meant nothing to me, but she welcomed us in Hindi. Her house was better than anything I'd ever seen, with rich-looking furniture, curtains and carpet – something like the photos in my red book. We sat at a dining table and I was presented for the first time with a knife and fork and taught how to use them correctly – I'd only ever eaten with my hands before. We also learned some table manners, such as not getting up and leaning over to reach for things, and sitting up straight. The visit to Aunty Ula's built up the excitement about the adventure we were about to embark upon.

We didn't receive any lessons in English, although at Nava Jeevan there was a pictorial alphabet wall chart, with 'A is for Apple' and so on. I think I was taught to say 'Hello', but there was no time for more than that – I was due to leave India almost immediately. I was leaving for a place I had been told was far away, at a distant end of the world. No-one ever talked about my coming back, and it seemed not to be of any concern.

Everyone agreed I was very lucky.

So I left India only a few days after I was told of my adoption (only a couple of months after I arrived the orphanage, which in today's more regulated processes would never happen). The six of us from Nava Jeevan who were flying to Australia, including my friend Asra, were joined by two more children, from a different orphanage, for the journey. After a stopover in Bombay (not yet known as Mumbai), we would fly first to Singapore and on to Melbourne, where our new families would meet us. Asra's new family lived in Victoria, and my new family, the Brierleys, were a second trip away, in Tasmania.

I was sad to learn that we were saying goodbye to Mrs Sood – three volunteer Australian women and a man from an

Australian government department would escort us on the flight. They were all very friendly, and although we couldn't communicate much, the excitement of the journey was enough to take away any worries.

I was over the moon when I finally boarded that huge plane. It seemed impossible that such a thing with so many seats and so many people could fly, but I don't remember being worried. We were each given a chocolate bar, an amazing luxury to me, which I carefully made last the entire journey. We talked and watched a film with headphones on. I was fascinated by the plug in the armrest and being in control of the channel and the volume. We ate everything we were given, under those little foil lids – the fact that people brought food to you seemed the start of a new life already. I guess we slept.

In Bombay, we stayed overnight in a hotel, which brought fresh amazement. It probably wasn't any more than a regular hotel in the West, but it was the most luxurious place I'd ever seen. The room smelled so fresh, and I had never slept in such a soft, clean bed in my life. Even with the excitement of everything that was happening, I had the best sleep I'd had for months. I marvelled at the bathroom, with its shiny shower and toilet. Around the hotel I saw more white people than I'd ever seen in one place, and, although it's embarrassing to admit it, all I remember thinking is that they looked so rich. There was so much that was new going on around me, I don't know if I thought about how I would soon be living with white people like them.

The next day, I was given a new pair of white shorts and a 'Tasmania' T-shirt, which had been sent by my new parents, to wear on the plane to Australia, and I was delighted with my outfit. Better still, we were taken to a toyshop nearby, where we were invited to choose a toy each – I guess there were limits on its extravagance, though I don't remember being told so. I still have the little car I chose, with its pullback mechanism that launched it across the room.

I know now that flying from Calcutta to Bombay had meant passing very close to my home town, 30 000 feet below. The plane I was on must have left one of those vapour trails I had watched with such fascination. I wonder if my mother unknowingly looked up at the right moment and saw my plane and its streaky trail. She would have been astonished beyond belief to know I was on board, and my destination.

5

A NEW LIFE

We landed in Melbourne on the night of 25 September 1987. Our group of kids was led by the escorts to a VIP area of the airport, where we were told our new families would be waiting to meet us.

I felt very shy as I walked into the room. There were lots of adults, all watching us as we came in, but I immediately recognised the Brierleys from the photos I had pored over in my red book. I tried to smile as I stood there, and looked down at the last bit of my precious chocolate bar in my hand. (The picture on the front of this book was taken when I first walked into the room in Melbourne – you can see the chocolate in my hand.)

An escort took me across the room and the first word I said to my new parents was 'Cadbury'. In India, Cadbury is synonymous with chocolate. And after we hugged, Mum got straight to work being a mother and produced a tissue to clean my hand.

Because I didn't speak much English, and my new mum and dad didn't speak any Hindi, we couldn't talk to each other. So instead we sat together and looked through the red book they'd sent me. Mum and Dad pointed out the house I would live in and the car we would drive there in, and we began to get used to each other's company, as much as we could. I suppose, too, I must have been a difficult child to reach – cautious and reserved after everything I'd been through. You can see that from my face in the pictures – not alarmed or anxious, especially, just a bit withdrawn, waiting to see what would happen. But despite all this, straightaway I knew I was safe with the Brierleys. It was just intuition – they had a quiet, kind manner and there was a warmth in their smiles that put me at ease.

I was also calmed by seeing Asra happily interacting with her family. She eventually left the airport with them, and I suppose we said goodbye in the cursory way children do. But my family had another short flight to make, from Melbourne over Bass Strait to Hobart. So our first night together was spent in the airport hotel, sharing a room.

Mum put me straight in the bath, lathering me up and dousing me to kill nits and the like. I was in a very different condition from kids in Australia. In addition to the external parasites, it turned out I had an intestinal tapeworm, broken teeth and a heart murmur (which happily didn't last). Being poor in India took its toll on your health, and living on the streets wore you out even more.

I slept soundly that first night in Australia – clearly I was getting used to hotels. When I woke the next morning, I saw Mum and Dad were watching me from their bed, waiting for me to stir. At first, I just looked out at them from under the sheets. Mum says she can still picture that morning clearly. She and Dad raised their heads from their double bed to peer across the room at the little mound of sheets in the single bed with a mop of black hair sticking out. And every now and then I would peep out at them. Afterwards, when I was still small and we'd recall that first night as a family, I'd remind them, 'I peeping, I peeping.'

I don't know that any of us could quite believe it was happening – that these strangers in the room were going to be my parents, or that this boy from India was going to be their son.

After breakfast, it was back on a plane for the short flight to Hobart, where I got a first look at my new country outside a hotel or airport. To eyes used to the crush and pollution of one of the most populous places on earth, it seemed so empty and so *clean* – the streets, the buildings, even the cars. There wasn't a soul to be seen as dark-coloured as me, but there was hardly anyone to see at all. It looked almost deserted.

As we drove through the unfamiliar countryside and into Hobart's suburbs, I saw a city of gleaming palaces, including my new home. I recognised it from the red book, but it looked even bigger and more impressive in reality. Inside there were four bedrooms for only three people, each of the rooms huge and so neat and clean. A carpeted living room, with comfortable couches and the biggest TV I'd ever seen, a bathroom with a big bath, a kitchen with shelves full of food. And a refrigerator: I loved standing in front of it just to feel the cold air come out whenever it was opened.

Best of all, though, was my bedroom – I'd never had a room to myself. Both houses I'd lived in in India were single rooms, and since then, of course, I'd been in dormitories with other children. But I don't remember being intimidated about sleeping on my own – perhaps my time sleeping on the streets had made me used to it. I was afraid of the dark, though, and required my bedroom door to be left open and a light on in the hall.

On my own soft bed, with a big map of India on the wall above it, there were new clothes, warm for the cool Tasmanian climate. And on the floor were boxes full of picture books and toys. It took me a little while to realise they were for me – all of them – and that I could look at them and play with them as I pleased. I felt cautious, maybe half-expecting some bigger kid to come along and take them. The idea of *having things* took some getting used to.

Nevertheless, for the most part adapting to the Western lifestyle seemed easy, with Mum and Dad's guidance, and they say I settled in well. At first we ate a lot of Indian food, and Mum slowly introduced me to an Australian diet. There were some big differences, and not just in taste: Mum remembers I noticed her putting red meat into the refrigerator once and ran up to her, crying, 'Cow, cow!' For a child brought up a Hindu, to slaughter the holy animal was taboo. For a moment she didn't know what to do, but then she smiled and said, 'No, no, it's beef.' Apparently that set my mind at rest. In the end, the delight I took in having abundant food close at hand overcame most matters of taste or culture.

One aspect of life in Australia that immediately appealed to me was experiencing life in the outdoors. In India, I was always in a town or city – often free to roam but nevertheless surrounded by buildings and roads and people. In Hobart, my parents were very active, taking me to play golf, birdwatching and sailing. Dad often took me out on his two-man catamaran, which only increased my love of the water, and I finally learned to swim. Just being able to look out at the horizon gave me peace of mind. India was so choked with development, you often couldn't see anything but the press of buildings around you – it was like being in a giant maze. Some people find the bustle of busy cities exciting and energising, but you see a different side of them if you're begging or trying to make people stop and listen to you. So, once I got used to it, I found the space in Hobart reassuring.

We lived in the suburb of Tranmere, across the river from central Hobart, and after about a month I started school in the next suburb, Howrah. Only years later did I realise the incredible coincidence. A couple of months before I arrived in Australia, I'd been surviving on the streets of Calcutta in an area also named Howrah, which gives its name to the city's huge railway station and famous bridge. The Hobart version is a pretty beachside suburb, with schools, sport clubs and a large shopping centre. It was apparently named in the 1830s by an English army officer who had served in the West Bengal capital and on coming to live in Hobart had seen something similar in the look of the hills and the river. If there was any resemblance then, it's lost now.

I loved school. There's no free education in India – I probably never would have made it to school without coming to the Tasmanian Howrah. Like the rest of the community, it was quite an Anglo-Saxon place, although there were a couple of kids from other countries. I had extra English lessons with one student from China and one also from India.

Although I'd become quite used to the change of colour and culture around me, as far as everyone else was concerned, of course, I stood out, especially as I had white parents. Other kids talked about their families and how they came from the country, or from Melbourne, and they would ask me where I was from, but all I could say was 'I'm from India.' But kids are curious – they wanted to know why I was here in a white family. Mum defused a lot of this by attending a parent and student day and telling them about my adoption. It seemed to satisfy my classmates and they didn't ask much after that.

I don't remember any racism at school. Mum, however, tells me there was some that I didn't understand properly. Perhaps that was the advantage to having to master the local language from scratch. Apparently, I once asked her, 'What's a "black basket?"' which upset her, and another time, as we were lining up for me to register for a sports team, Dad heard the woman in front of him say, 'I don't want him in the same team as that black boy.' I don't mean to make light of comments like that, but in comparison with what I've heard about other non-Anglos' experiences, I don't think I had it too bad, and I've always felt that I grew up without any scars from racism.

That might not have be true for Mum and Dad. I'm told we did attract some negative attention at the local Indian Cultural

Society, which conducted dinners and dances. There was quite a large Indian community in Hobart, from Fiji and South Africa as well as India itself, and for a time we went along and enjoyed the society's events. But my parents came to notice that we were treated a little suspiciously, and determined that it was considered somehow wrong for an Indian child to be taken from India by white parents. Needless to say, I was oblivious to all this.

Another organisation we were involved in was ASIAC, the Australian Society for Intercountry Aid (Children), which helped people adopt from overseas. Mum became very active, helping other Australian families with the constantly changing processes, as well as the personal challenges. Through that organisation, I met other children who'd come to Australia from elsewhere and now lived in mixed-race families. Mum tells me that at our first ASIAC picnic I seemed surprised – and perhaps a little put out – to discover I wasn't the only 'special one' in Hobart. Despite that humbling life lesson, I made friends, one of whom was Ravi, another Indian boy, who lived with his new family in Launceston, and our families visited each other often during those early years.

ASIAC also put me back in touch with some of the other kids from Nava Jeevan. My closest friend, Asra, had ended up with a family in the riverside Victorian town of Winchelsea, and our families had kept us in phone contact. A year after I arrived, all of us met up in Melbourne with two of the other kids who had been adopted into Australia, Abdul and Musa, for a trip to the zoo. I was overjoyed to see familiar faces, and we all busily compared notes on our new lives, measuring them against our time in the orphanage together. Although it hadn't been a terrible place, I don't think any of us wished ourselves back there. It seemed to me that each of them was as happy as I was.

Later the same year, Mrs Sood herself arrived in Hobart, escorting another new adoptee, Asha, whom I remembered from the orphanage. It made me happy to see Mrs Sood again – she'd taken good care of us, and until I left India was probably the most friendly and trustworthy person I met after becoming lost. I like to think that for her part it must have been satisfying to see some of the children she'd helped in their new environments. Mrs Sood dealt with a huge amount of trauma among her charges, but I've always thought the rewards must have been equally large. Some adoptions mightn't have worked out as well as mine, but occasionally visiting the children she'd connected with new families must have given Mrs Sood the energy she needed to return to her work.

When I was ten, Mum and Dad adopted a second child from India. I was keen on the idea of having a sibling. In fact, it seemed that the person I missed most from India was my sister, to the point that when I was asked what I wanted for Christmas, I would sometimes say, 'I want Shekila back.' Of course, I missed my mother deeply, but, from the first, Mum had done a brilliant job of being a mother to me, and having a father's attention made me very happy. They couldn't replace being with my birth mother, but they did lessen the loss as much as they could. The one person really absent from my life, especially for someone used to being left for long periods without any parent around, was a brother or sister.

Shekila had been my special responsibility. She was the member of the family I was most closely bonded with, and most haunted by – Mum remembers me sometimes saying I felt guilty for not looking after her as well as I might have done. Perhaps I particularly had in mind the night I left with Guddu.

When Mum and Dad had applied to adopt the first time, they hadn't put any gender conditions or restrictions of any kind on their application. They were happy to have whatever child needed a home; that's how they got me. So they did exactly the same thing the second time. We might have acquired a young girl, or a child older than me, but as it happened, we got my little brother, Mantosh.

I didn't care that he wasn't a sister – the idea of having another child to play with at home was enough for me.

And – assuming he'd be rather quiet and shy like me – I thought I could help him adjust to this new life. He'd be someone for me to help look after.

But Mantosh and I were very different, partly because of the natural differences between people, but also because of our different experiences in India. It's one of the things that makes people who adopt children, especially from abroad, so brave: often the kids they're taking in come with troubled backgrounds, having suffered in ways that make adjusting to their new life difficult, and which can be hard to understand and even harder to help. I was reticent and reserved; Mantosh, at least at first, was loud and disobedient. I wanted to please; he rebelled.

What we did have in common was that Mantosh's background had a lot of unknowns in it too. He'd also grown up poor and with no formal education, and can't say for sure exactly where or when he was born. He arrived as a nine-year-old with no birth certificate, medical records or any official documentation of his origins. We celebrate his birthday on 30 November, because that's the day he landed in Australia. Like me, it was as if he simply fell to earth, but, lucky for him, he landed in the care of the Brierleys in Hobart.

The story we now know is this: Mantosh was born somewhere in or near Calcutta and grew up speaking Bengali. His mother fled their violent family home, leaving him behind, and he was sent to live with his frail grandmother. But as she couldn't even look after herself properly, much less a little boy as well, she handed him over to the state and eventually he ended up in the care of ISSA, Mrs Sood's adoption agency, just as I had. The legal process permitted an orphan to live in an ISSA orphanage for two months while attempts were made to restore them to their family or arrange an adoption. Mrs Sood was excited by the idea of placing him with the Brierleys, so we would become brothers.

But Mantosh didn't enjoy the same smooth process of adoption as I had. Because he *did* have parents, even though he couldn't return to them – his mother's whereabouts were unknown and his father didn't want him – there were complications in the attempts to make him available for adoption. With his two months exhausted, he had to be transferred back to Liluah – the intimidating juvenile home I had been sent to – while ISSA continued to try to arrange his adoption by Mum and Dad. At Liluah, Mantosh wasn't as lucky as I was. He was physically and sexually abused. Later, it emerged that in the past he'd been shockingly abused by his uncles as well.

It took two years for the complex legal procedures to be worked through, by which time he'd obviously been scarred terribly by his experiences. The only positive was that he'd learned more English than I had, which helped him when he arrived in

Australia. What happened to Mantosh exposed the harm that the bureaucratic adoption system can do. When I learned about his past, later on, I couldn't stop thinking about the nights I'd spent in the Liluah juvenile home, and how easily what happened to my brother could have happened to me.

When Mantosh first arrived, he didn't seem completely sure what adoption meant – he didn't seem to understand that his move here was permanent. The situation might not have been explained to him clearly enough, or he just wasn't as certain as I had been that this was the right thing to do. When he began to understand that he wasn't going back to India, he had mixed feelings – the sort of ambivalence that's understandable in all adoptions, and which I had experienced myself, although to a much lesser extent. That was compounded by an emotional volatility doubtless caused by his traumas. When he was young he could become explosively angry without any obvious provocation, and though he was an emaciated little boy, he could be as strong as a man. I'd never experienced anything like it, and unfortunately it made me somewhat wary of him when we were little. Mum and Dad were patient and loving, but firm, and both Mantosh and I think all the more of them for their determination to make a family out of the four of us.

Still, although I understand things now, at the time I was unsettled. Because of the difficulties he was going through, Mantosh required most of our parents' attention. I was reasonably well adjusted by then, but I still needed reassurance that I was loved and cared for. Jealousy of a sibling receiving more attention at home is normal, but Mantosh and I both had insecurities from our pasts that probably made us react more strongly than most. As a result, I even ran away from home one night soon after Mantosh arrived. It was a measure of how much I'd changed – and how much I'd learned about the resilience and underlying love in a family – that I didn't try living on the streets again. Much more typical of a Western kid testing his parents' commitment to him, I made it to the local bus depot around the corner. I soon got cold and hungry and went home. Still, although Mantosh and I had our differences, we also went swimming and fishing together, and played cricket and rode our bikes, like any young brothers.

Mantosh didn't enjoy school as much as I did. He was frustrated and disruptive in class, although he at least shared my enthusiasm for sport. Unlike me, he seemed to attract racist comments, to which he would retaliate and then find himself in trouble. That seemed to spur on his bullies, who would make a game of stirring him up. Unfortunately, the teachers seemed ill-equipped to assist someone struggling with adjusting to a new way of life. But it didn't help that initially Mantosh wasn't used to accepting direction from women in authority, a prejudice learned from his family in India. I'd had to learn some of these cultural differences, too. Mum remembers taking me somewhere in the car once and hearing me sulkily say, 'Lady no drive.' She pulled over and said, 'Lady no drive, boy walk!' I quickly learned my lesson.

I know Mum feels some regret that, because Mantosh needed so much of my parents' attention, I spent more time than I might have otherwise left to my own devices. But other than causing the odd tantrum, it didn't much bother me, perhaps because that's what I was used to in India. I liked my independence. And we still did plenty of things together as a family – we would go to a restaurant every Friday as a family outing, and took trips away during school holidays.

At one point, Mum and Dad planned a major family trip – to travel to India together. At first, I was extremely enthusiastic about it, and Mantosh seemed to like the idea too – we'd always been surrounded by Indian things and thought a lot about the country, so we all talked excitedly about what we'd see and where we'd go. Of course, neither of us knew where our home towns were, so we'd visit other places and learn more about the country we were from.

But as the date of the trip neared, we both began to feel

anxious. There was no avoiding the fact that our memories of India weren't happy ones, and the more real the prospect of going back there became, the more vivid those memories seemed to be. A lot of things that we'd been able to put behind us – or at least put from our minds – returned in Hobart. I certainly didn't want to go back to Calcutta, and I began to be agitated that any other place we visited might turn out to be my home, or somewhere I would recognise. I still wanted to find my other mother, but I was happy where I was – I wanted both things. It was confusing and increasingly upsetting. And maybe subconsciously I was worried about getting lost again. I can only imagine what must have been going through Mantosh's mind.

In the end our parents decided that the trip would stir up too many emotions, and it was better for the moment to let sleeping dogs lie.

6

MY MUM'S JOURNEY

I couldn't write about my journey without explaining how my parents came to make their choice to adopt two children from India. And not two specific children – as I've mentioned, unusually for Western adopting parents, they were prepared to give a home to whichever two children they were sent, of any gender, age or circumstance. That seems to me a particularly remarkable and selfless act, and how they came to do it is part of my story.

My mum – Sue – was born on the north-west coast of Tasmania, to parents who had emigrated from central Europe after World War Two. They'd both had rough times growing up.

Her mother, Julie, was born in Hungary, in a poor family of fourteen children. Julie's father went off to work in Canada as a lumberjack, with the intention of sending back money, but he never returned, abandoning his wife and all their children. The older children tried to help out as best they could, but when the war came most of the brothers were taken away to fight and died in battle. By the time the Russians arrived in Hungary, pursuing the retreating Nazis, Julie's family had fled into Germany, and didn't return. (When the fighting ended in Hungary, some of the villagers who had also been displaced tried to go back to their homes, but Julie's family decided it was too dangerous. Many Hungarians who did return found Russians living in their homes, and when they tried to reclaim them they were shot down in the streets.) Julie was just nineteen years old as the war was drawing to an end.

Mum's father, Josef, was Polish and had a traumatic childhood of his own. When he was five years old his mother died and his father took a new wife. His stepmother hated Josef so much it's said she tried to poison him, and he was eventually sent away to be brought up by his grandmother. Mum says that because of his stepmother, his grandmother raised him with a deep bitterness against women.

When Nazi Germany invaded Poland at the start of the war, Josef joined the Resistance and took part in bombing and shooting missions, but became deeply disturbed by what he experienced. Finally, despite his role in the Resistance, he fled the advancing Russians too, and also ended up in Germany.

Josef was a good-looking man – literally tall, dark and handsome – and when Julie met him, in the chaos of the tail end of the war, she fell in love. They married, and had a baby, Mary, by the time the war was over. It was a turbulent period, with displaced people on the roads and trains all across Europe, and the couple wanted to travel to the new world to start over. They managed to get themselves to Italy, and boarded a ship they thought would take them to Canada, but it ended up sailing to Australia. So, like a good number of refugees, they ended up in a place they hadn't chosen, but had to make the best of it.

Julie spent at least a year in the infamous Victorian migrant camp at Bonegilla, near Albury-Wodonga, taking care of the baby, while Josef was contracted to build houses in Tasmania and lived on his own at a work camp. The idea was that he would send for them when he had a place suitable for a family – something that must have reminded Julie about her father – but Josef was as good as his word, and when the opportunity came up to share a farm with another family outside the town of Somerset, near Burnie, Josef and Julie were reunited. Josef worked hard, and before long he bought the farm next door and built their own cottage. Mary was six when Mum was born, in 1954.

Sixteen months later, she had a younger sister too, Christine.

Like many survivors of the war, Josef had been left psychologically disturbed, which became more apparent as the years went on. Mum's early upbringing was very harsh, especially because of her father's moods, which swung between melancholia, rage and violence. She describes him as a big, powerful man, and a frightening one. He came from a background in which beating wives and children was commonplace.

Polish to the core, Josef drank a lot of vodka, every day, and also insisted on unvarying traditional meals of pan-fried pork with cabbage and potatoes. Mum hated it, and became an emaciated and unhealthy child. She says to this day it still makes her feel queasy to talk about what they had to eat.

Josef made a considerable amount of money through his building business and acquired a lot of property. Mum thinks he might even have been Somerset's first millionaire, although no-one is sure exactly how much he was worth. Unfortunately, as his condition worsened, he became delusional and deranged, and was notorious for his bad business dealings. He also refused to pay rates and taxes on his properties. It might have had something to do with his mental health, or that he refused to recognise civic authority, but he simply would not pay up. It led to his downfall and broke up the family.

*

My Mum grew up quickly and managed to lift herself out of her difficult circumstances. She left school in Year 10, when her father insisted she get a job, and started work in Burnie as a pharmacy assistant. Her wage gave her some independence for the first time in her life. She earned around fifteen dollars a week, two dollars of which she was proud to give her mother for her board. She used most of the rest to assemble a glory box, with everything she might need for the married life she hoped would come. At sixteen, after years of stress and undernourishment at home, she felt like her life had turned around at last.

One day, on a lunch break with a couple of her girlfriends, Mum noticed a young man who was up 'all the way' from Hobart – a visitor from the capital was news in Burnie. His name was John Brierley. He later asked the girls about their friend Sue, and not long afterwards she had a phone call from him, inviting her out.

John was a 24-year-old handsome surfie, blond and tanned, polite and easygoing. His English father was a British Airways pilot who had retired at fifty and emigrated with his family to the warmer climate of Australia. The teenage John hadn't been too sure about leaving England at first, but once he got out to Australia and into the sun and surf lifestyle there was no looking back for him. Dad hasn't been back to England since.

Mum hadn't been interested in relationships before she met

Dad, largely due to her experiences of her father. It was only when her older sister, Mary, met her own husband-to-be that Mum first encountered a man who was decent and respectful, and who wouldn't beat his wife and children. It helped her see that some men could be trusted.

In 1971, a year after they met, Dad was offered a promotion which would require transferring to the mainland, but rather than leave Mum behind he stayed in Tasmania and proposed. They were married on a Saturday, moved to a small flat in Hobart, and Mum started work on the Monday at a pharmacy there. It was as if he had turned up on a white horse, swept her off her feet, and the next thing they were married and living together. With hard work and saving, they bought a block of land in the waterside suburb of Tranmere and started building, and in 1975 Mum turned twenty-one in her own home.

Though Mum managed to leave Burnie, her family's fortunes worsened, which affected her deeply. Her father, Josef, went bankrupt twice. The second time was for the sake of a $500 tax fine he refused to pay. He was sent to the Burnie lock-up until his debts were cleared. Mum and the rest of the family didn't know it then, but he had thousands of dollars secretly stashed in the house, which could have bailed him out, had he told them about it.

It was the beginning of a downward spiral. The accountant

appointed by the court held a fire sale to retrieve a few thousand dollars in outstanding taxes and the fine, and then claimed more than the revenue raised for his fee, leaving the family with its old debt and a new one to the accountant. When Mum was around thirty, Josef was hauled off to prison in Hobart, where, clearly suffering from alcohol withdrawal on top of everything else, he became excessively violent and was transferred to a psychiatric prison.

There, Josef borrowed money from a loan shark who in less than a year managed to take his remaining property in interest repayments, leaving the family with nothing. Mum's mother finally left her volatile husband a year later; Josef, still in prison, threatened to kill her, blaming her for everything. She moved into a flat, where she suffered illness caused by a nearby toxic paper mill, until Mum – by this time mother to two adopted sons – was able to bring her to join us in Hobart. Mantosh and I enjoyed having our gran close by. Though Josef had been discharged by then, Mum didn't want to expose Mantosh and me to his troubled nature, and we never met him. He died when I was twelve.

Mum's hard times made her strong-willed and determined, and gave her different priorities from others she knew. The early years of her marriage were a time of change in Australia: the Whitlam Government was voted in, after the upheavals of the Sixties, and the social and political landscape was being transformed. Even though Mum and Dad weren't exactly hippies, they were attracted to the 'alternative' ideas being discussed.

People were particularly worried about overpopulation, and there was a growing concern about the impact of so many billions of people on the world's environment. There were other issues too, including war. Dad was fortunate to have not been sent to fight in Vietnam. Their progressive views helped Mum form the idea that one way to make a difference was to adopt children in need from developing countries.

Because of all she'd been through growing up, Mum had decided that there was nothing sacrosanct about families being formed by birth. Though brought up Catholic, in a culture where women were expected to have children, she and Dad thought the world had enough people in it already, with so many millions of children in dire need. They agreed that there were other ways to create a family beyond having children themselves.

There was also an amazing personal moment in Mum's past that she says put her on the path to her non-traditional family. When she was about twelve years old, the pressures from her family's issues led her to something like a breakdown, during which she had what she can only describe as a 'vision'. It left her feeling like an electric shock had gone through her. The vision was of a brown-skinned child standing by her side – she sensed it so keenly she could even feel the child's warmth. It was so striking she wondered about her sanity, and even whether it was possible she'd seen a ghost. But as time went by, she became more comfortable with her vision, and came to accept it as something precious, a visitation of some sort that only she knew about. It was the first time in her bleak life that she'd experienced an overwhelming feeling of something good, and she held on to it.

As a young married adult, with a like-minded husband, she had the chance to make her vision come true. So, although they could have had children themselves, Mum and Dad agreed that they would adopt children from poor countries, and give them the home and loving family they needed. Dad admits that Mum was the driving force in their decision to adopt. In fact, Mum says that she felt so strongly about it that if they hadn't agreed on it, it might have been the end of the marriage. But Dad was more than happy with their plan, and once they'd made the decision they never wavered.

They were, though, given plenty of cause to rethink. As soon as they started making official enquiries, they hit a problem –

under Tasmanian state law at the time, couples who could conceive weren't permitted to adopt. For the time being, that was simply that. They didn't change their principles; instead, they chose to sponsor children in need overseas (as they still do) and otherwise enjoy their own good fortune childlessly, dining out, sailing and taking holidays every year.

Adopting always remained at the back of their minds, however. There was obviously no biological clock ticking for them, and the other time constraint at the time – specifying a maximum age difference of forty years between the youngest adopting parent and the child, to avoid young children being adopted by elderly people who might struggle to take care of them – was unlikely to affect them, as they hadn't requested a child of any particular age.

Sixteen years passed after their resolution to adopt. Then one day, Mum met a beautiful little brown-skinned girl, Maree, who had been adopted by a local family who also had a biological son. Mum realised that meant the law preventing fertile parents from adopting must have been changed. She felt the hairs go up on the back of her neck – she had an uncanny feeling that this girl could have been the child by her side in her vision as a twelve-year-old. It prompted her to enquire about adoption again, and to her joy she confirmed that she and Dad could now apply to adopt children from overseas. Despite having long before established the rhythms of their life, they had no hesitation in starting the process.

After many interviews, lots of document preparations and police checks, they were approved to adopt. Then they had to choose a country to send their file to. They had heard from an adoption group in Victoria that the agency ISSA, in Calcutta, had a humanitarian focus and acted more quickly than elsewhere to place needy Indian children in new homes. Mum had always been fascinated by India and knew something about the conditions many people were living under there: in 1987 Australia's population was 17 million, and that same year in India, around 14 million children under the age of ten died from illness or starvation. While obviously adopting one child was merely a drop in the ocean, it was something they could do. And it would make a huge difference to that one child. They chose India.

Some adoptive parents wait ten years for a child that meets their conditions: they might want a baby to raise from infancy, or specifically a boy or a girl, or a particular age. Mum and Dad felt it was an important part of their stance that they offered help to whoever needed it, rather than someone picked on the basis of their preferences. So they simply said they wanted 'a child'.

The motto of ISSA, run by the wonderful Mrs Saroj Sood,

is: 'Somewhere a child is waiting. Somewhere a family is waiting. We at ISSA bring them together.' And in our case it really was as simple as that. Only a few weeks after their application Mum and Dad received a call to say they had been allocated a child named Saroo, who didn't know his surname or anything else much about his origins. Mum says that from the moment they saw a copy of the picture ISSA had taken for a court document, they felt I was theirs.

Mum was delighted when the word came through, but also calm: somewhere inside her, she'd always felt that the vision she'd had at the age of twelve had meant it was her destiny to have an adopted child by her side. It seemed like fate had required them to wait sixteen years after deciding to adopt for me to be ready and waiting for them. Then things happened quickly: it was only seven months after they applied to adopt, and scarcely three months after their approval, that I arrived.

Mum believes that helping children from harsh circumstances in other countries – through sponsorship or adoption – is something more Australians should think about doing. The stress of the bureaucratic problems that delayed Mantosh's adoption affected her very badly; in fact, she became dangerously ill as a result. She is an advocate of replacing Australia's various state laws on inter-country adoption with a simplified federal law. She's critical of governments making it too difficult, and feels that if it was a little easier maybe more families would do it.

Mum's story makes me feel impossibly lucky, even blessed. She became stronger because of her tough childhood, and has taken those experiences and made something worthwhile out of them. I hope to be able to do the same, as, I'm sure, does Mantosh. Mum's understanding about terrible childhoods made her a terrific mother to the children she adopted, and also an inspiration to us as adults. I love her for the person she is, but above all I respect her for the way she's gone about her life and the decisions she and Dad made. Certainly, I'll always be profoundly grateful, to both my parents, for the life they've given me.

7

GROWING UP

By the time I began high school, the map of India was still on my wall, but I hardly noticed it next to my posters of the Red Hot Chili Peppers. I was growing up Australian – a proud Tassie.

Of course, I hadn't forgotten my past or stopped thinking about my Indian family. I was still determined not to forget any detail of my childhood memories, and often went through them in my head, as though telling myself a story. I prayed my mother was still alive and well. Sometimes I would lie in bed, visualising the streets of my home town, seeing myself walking home through them, opening the door and watching over my mother and Shekila as they slept. Transported there in my mind, I would concentrate on sending them a message that I was okay and they shouldn't worry. It was almost a meditation. But these memories were the background of my life, not the forefront. I dived in to my teenage years pretty much as any other kid might.

At secondary school there were a lot more kids from other ethnic backgrounds than in primary school, particularly Greeks, Chinese and other Indians, so any difference I had felt dissolved. I made good friends, joined a school rock band as guitarist, and still played lots of sport, particularly soccer, swimming and athletics. And because the high school was quite small, it helped Mantosh settle down too.

I remained pretty independent, though, and did my own thing. By the age of fourteen, I was running off to the local pier with my friends to fool around and drink on the sly. I had a girlfriend soon, too. I wouldn't say I was particularly wild, but I was spending more and more time goofing off. It's tempting to attribute this stage of my life to my childhood and adoption, but frankly I think I just got swept away in the things that most teenagers discover.

I'd never been particularly academic, but my school marks began to suffer with all my extracurricular pursuits, both sporting and social. And eventually I came up against the limit of my parents' tolerance. Mum and Dad were determined, hardworking people, and it seemed to them that I was coasting along a little aimlessly. They gave me an ultimatum: leave school before Year 12 and get a job (as Mantosh later chose); work hard and get into university; or join the armed forces.

This was a shock. The idea of the military alarmed me, as was exactly the intention. It sounded like an institutional life too reminiscent of the homes for lost children that I wanted to put behind me. The proposition also had a more positive effect – it reminded me of how badly I'd wanted to learn when I was in India. I'd been given a life I couldn't have imagined, and I was certainly enjoying it, but maybe I wasn't making the most of it.

That was incentive enough to knuckle down: from then on I became a model student, shutting myself in my room after school to review the lessons, improving my marks and even lifting myself to the top of some classes. Once I finished school, I chose a three-year accounting diploma at TAFE, with a view to using that to leverage entrance to university. I also got a job in hospitality.

After that initial wake-up call, Mum and Dad didn't put pressure on me to follow any particular path, and they never made me feel that I owed them anything for adopting me. As long as I was applying myself, they would support my decisions. They would have been pleased to see me finish the diploma, but, instead of going on to university, I found I was enjoying the money and sociability of hospitality work so much that I was happy to leave accounting behind. For several years, I combined work and play – I had various jobs in bars, clubs and restaurants around Hobart, and these were good times, spinning bottles like in the film *Cocktail* and promoting band nights. But when I saw my work peers getting stuck in the business with no prospects, I knew I wanted more. I decided to get a qualification in hospitality management, which I hoped would lead to more senior roles, and was fortunate enough to receive a scholarship to go to the Australian International Hotel School in Canberra. Because of my on-the-job experience, they knocked a three-year course back to a year and a half.

Although at the time I was still living at home, I was usually working, studying or at my girlfriend's house, so the prospect of moving out wasn't a momentous one. I think my parents were pleased I was taking the initiative. So it seemed a natural step for us all when I packed my bags and moved to Canberra.

As it turned out, it was the best decision I could have made. It was in Canberra that my mind was unexpectedly turned again to India and I began to think about how I might search for my childhood home.

When I moved into a hall of residence at the college in Canberra in 2007, I quickly discovered that not only were there a lot of international students, but that they were mostly Indian. The majority were from Delhi and what were by then known as Mumbai and Kolkata.

I'd known other Indian kids at high school, but like me they'd grown up in Australia. Getting to know this group of people was a completely different experience. They spoke English with me, but among themselves they spoke Hindi, the first I'd heard in years. My first language was almost completely forgotten – the Indians at high school had only spoken English too – and so initially I experienced a kind of reverse culture shock. In the company of the international students I was for the first time stripped of my Indianness – rather than being somewhat exotic, I was the Australian among the Indians.

I was drawn to them for the basic reason that they were from the same place as me, some of them from the very city in which I'd been lost. They had trod the same streets and been on the same trains. They responded to my interest in them and welcomed me into their social circles. It was with this group of people that, at the age of twenty-six, I began for the first time genuinely to explore being Indian. I don't mean in a political or academic way, or in the awkward manner of the well-meaning associations my parents had tried out. I mean I began to feel comfortable just living in the Indian students' culture and company. We'd eat Indian food and go clubbing together, take trips to nearby towns or gather at someone's house to watch Hindi masala movies, those wonderful Bollywood blends of action, romance, comedy and drama. It wasn't false or forced; it was just a natural way of being. And the people I met weren't associated with adoption agencies or trauma. They were just regular people who happened to be Indian. They encouraged me to relearn some of my native tongue, and I also found out something of the rapid changes that had gone on in modernising India.

In turn, I told them my own story. It was completely different describing my time in the train station when the people I was talking with knew it as Kolkata's massive Howrah Station, and the river next to it as the Hooghly River. They were astonished, especially those from Kolkata, who understood something of the life I had led. And I'm sure it seemed incredible that someone from that background was now in halls with them in Canberra.

Two things happened as a result of these conversations. Firstly, my past became much more present than it had seemed in years. Although I always kept my memories intact by going over them in my head, I'd not spoken about them much for a long time. I'd told the odd person, mainly girlfriends, but very few – not because I was ashamed of it, or wanted to keep it a secret, but just because it didn't seem that important anymore. Each time I told someone, there were a lot of questions that had to be answered, and I felt it changed their view of me in much more fundamental ways than it deserved – I became Saroo-who-used-to-live-on-the-streets-in-Calcutta, rather than just Saroo, and mostly I just wanted to be Saroo. Now I was telling people who knew the places I was talking about, which was different. I'm sure it changed their view of me, but usually to increase the understanding between us, rather than open up a gap. And to talk about it like this brought it more to the front of my mind. Telling other Australian people had been a little abstract, as though talking about a fairytale, however much they sympathised and tried to imagine what it had been like. Telling these people, who had firsthand experience of the same places, made it much more real.

Secondly, telling my story to people actually from India brought out the detectives in them. The whereabouts of my home town was a mystery they wanted to solve, and they asked me lots of questions about what I could remember. Through their eyes, for the first time since I was in Howrah Station, I saw the possibility of working it out. Here was a bunch of people who knew the country well – the adults I'd needed when I was first lost. Maybe they could help me now.

So I tried out my meagre collection of clues on my friends. It was the first time for many, many years that I had conjured up my ignorant five-year-old's understanding of the geography of my childhood. There was Ginestlay, which might have been the name of my town, but which might equally have been the area or even the street. And then there was the nearby station where

I'd boarded the train alone, called something like 'Berampur'.

I reminded my friends that the Kolkata authorities had tried and failed to work out my origins with these fragments, but they still thought it was a good start. I admitted I was hazy on exactly how long I'd been stuck on the train, but that I was certain I had boarded at night and thought I had arrived in Kolkata the next day before noon – it was certainly daytime. Although traumatic experiences such as those I'd had living on the streets seemed to be imprinted on my mind with great detail, the first big trauma – being trapped alone on a train, realising I was powerless to stop my being taken away from home – appeared instead to have overwhelmed me. I recalled it more in snapshots of distress. But I had always felt that I had probably travelled for between twelve and fifteen hours.

One of my friends, a girl called Amreen, said she would ask her father, who worked for Indian Railways in New Delhi, if he knew of places with the names I remembered, probably about half a day away from Kolkata. I was excited and agitated – this was as close as I'd ever been to the help I'd been looking for on the railway platforms twenty years before.

A week later, he responded: he had never heard of Ginestlay, but there was a suburb of Kolkata called Brahmapur, a city called Baharampur in a more remote region of the same eastern state of West Bengal, and a city in the state of Orissa, down the east coast, formerly known as Berhampur and now also named Brahmapur. The first one – the suburb actually in Kolkata – was obviously not the one. But it made me wonder why no-one I'd asked at Howrah Station had thought this was the place I was after. Maybe my pronunciation was wrong. Or else they didn't pause for long enough to listen to what I was saying.

The second and third places didn't seem much more likely. I didn't think they were far enough away from Howrah Station for the journey I'd been on, although I supposed it was possible I'd been on a circuitous route. The Orissan city was less than ten kilometres from the east coast, but I'd never seen the ocean until I flew over it to Australia – I'd once gone on a memorable trip to watch the sun set over a lake not far from my home town, but the sight of the open sea below the plane astonished me. Could I have grown up so close to the coast but never known it? On the other hand, my friends thought that, based on the way I looked, I might come from West Bengal. That reminded me that when I was growing up in Hobart, Mum had told me some elderly Indians we met had also thought it likely I came from the east. Could I be remembering the train journey wrongly? Might the time and distance have been exaggerated in the mind of a frightened five-year-old? Little seeds of doubt were being sown in my mind.

*

In addition to the hunches of my friends, I started to use the internet to search for more information. We'd had internet at home since my later years at school, but it was a very different medium from what it is today. It was much slower, of course, especially in the pre-broadband dial-up days, but what we call the internet now was only just getting started as 'the web' when I was finishing school. Tools like Wikipedia were only in their infancy by the time I started college. Today, it's hard to imagine that you could fail to turn up information on any topic imaginable, no matter how obscure, but it wasn't long ago that the internet was more the preserve of geeks and academics.

This was also before social media, when it was much less easy or common to connect with people you didn't already know. Email was a more formal communication tool, not something with which you could reach out anonymously to the world. Adding that to the fact that I wasn't thinking much about my Indian past, it just hadn't crossed my mind before that this reasonably new invention could be of some use to me.

At college, as well as some encouraging Indian friends, I had 24-hour access to the internet and my own computer on a desk in my room. So I started searching for any kind of information I could find using various spellings of 'Ginestlay', with no success – at least, nothing that I could make sense of. The 'Berampur'-type names were similarly inconclusive – too many possibilities and nothing much to go on.

If I'd begun to have doubts about my memories of these names and the length of time I was on the train, I had none about my memories of my family, or the town and the streets I'd walked as a child. And I could close my eyes and see clearly the train station in Berampur where I climbed aboard the train, for example: the position of the platform, the big pedestrian over-pass at one end, and the large water tower on its high platform towering above. I knew that if I could just see any of the places that had been suggested by my friends and the internet, or if I could somehow see what someone thought was my home town, I could tell straight away if it was the one. It was the names that I couldn't be sure of.

Maps didn't help. I knew that somewhere among all the names and lines was my home, if only I knew the right place to look, but the only maps I could find weren't big enough to show small villages, let alone neighbourhoods or the detailed street plans I needed. All I could do was look for names that seemed similar, scanning likely areas based on their proximity to Kolkata and my own appearance. But even if I found a town name similar to Berampur or Ginestlay, it would be impossi-ble to verify whether it was relevant to me. This place? Who knows? How could I tell if our tumbledown dwelling or the right train station was there? For a while I even toyed with the idea of flying to West Bengal to search on the ground, but not very seriously. For how long could I possibly ramble through parts of the country looking for something familiar? The place was enormous. It was too much like jumping on random trains at Howrah Station.

Then, I became aware of a map that actually *would* allow me to roam across the landscape, and it could be done from the security of my study chair: Google Earth.

Many people probably remember their first experience of Google Earth. Its satellite imaging meant anyone could look at the world, from above, sweeping across it like an astronaut. You could view whole continents, countries or cities, or search for place names, and then zoom down on the spots you were interested in, rendered in astonishing detail – up close to the Eiffel Tower, or Ground Zero, or your own house. In fact, that seemed to be what everyone typically did first – zeroed in on where they lived and saw what it looked like from above, like a bird or a god. When I heard what Google Earth could do, my heart raced. Might my childhood home be visible, if I worked out where to look? Google Earth could have been invented for me – the perfect tool. I got on my computer and began searching.

As I'd never got even a flicker of recognition from anyone about Ginestlay, I thought that the place sounding like Berampur was the most solid reference I had. And if I found it, my home town would be close by along the train line. So I searched for places like Berampur and, as always, the results were numerous – there was a large number of variations of the name strung across the length and breadth of India, and multiple places sharing some of them. Brahmapur, Baharampur, Berhampur, Berhampore, Birampur, Burumpur, Burhampoor, Brahmpur . . . on and on they went.

It seemed sensible to start with the two places Amreen's father had suggested, in West Bengal and Orissa. Slowly but surely, aerial images of each town appeared on the screen – the way Google Earth worked was exactly as I'd hoped. With this tool, I would be able to see any landmarks I remembered, and hopefully identify the right place almost as easily as if I was there in person, or, at least, as if I was there in a hot air balloon – looking down at a place from above meant twisting your mind a little to imagine it from the street.

Baharampur in West Bengal had a couple of train stations, but they didn't have the overpass I distinctly remembered, and there didn't appear to be any place on the lines out of town with a name like Ginestlay, either. One line also ran close to several large lakes that I was sure would be visible from a train, and I'd never seen anything like them where I'd been. In fact, the surroundings of the town didn't seem right at all – the place I was looking for had a range of hills nearby that the train line ran through, which I couldn't see close to this place, and everything looked too green and lush. The region I came from was a patchwork of farmland around dusty towns. I had to concede that changes could have occurred since my time there – maybe more irrigation had been brought in and the region had become greener. But the other factors seemed to rule it out.

The city in Orissa, Brahmapur, seemed in a drier region, but its station had very long covered platforms on either side of the tracks, which was different from the simpler configuration I was looking for. There was no water tower to be seen, either; instead, there were lots of silos of some kind, which I surely would have remembered. Once again there was no Ginestlay along the lines near this place. And seeing an image of how close the sea was to the city made me certain I couldn't have been unaware of it.

That neither of these looked right was no reason to give up hope – there were many, many other places to look at – but it was disheartening. And it made me consider how much things might have changed since I'd been there. Stations might have been refurbished or rebuilt, roads changed nearby, towns grown. If too much had changed, I might not find it easy to recognise the station I was looking for after all.

Despite the comprehensive nature of this new resource – or because of it – it was clear that searching for my home was going to be a mammoth task. If I wasn't certain about the place names,

I couldn't rely on the search function to deliver the answer. And even if I stumbled upon the right area, perhaps I wouldn't be able to recognise it from the air. How could I be certain about anything? On top of all that, internet speeds and computers were much slower then – Google Earth was an incredible tool, but a massive one, and using it to look over great distances would be hugely time-consuming.

If I was going to take my studies seriously, I wouldn't be able to spend all my time scouring Google Earth. So, after the initial excitement, I told myself I was just mucking about and tried not to get too distracted by it. I put some time into checking out a few places, concentrating on the north-east regions around Kolkata, for several months on and off. But I didn't find anything familiar.

For a while, some of my friends got used to me announcing that I'd given up the search, only to admit later that it was still playing on my mind. Many of the original Indian sleuths had returned home and others let the issue go when it seemed I might not be as troubled by it as they had first thought.

Eventually, I let the whole thing slide. The quest started to seem a little abstract. It was hard to feel I was getting anywhere – I was searching for the needle in the haystack, and the task seemed beyond the commitment I could give it. I was at college to study, which required a great deal of my attention, and

I didn't want to become a hermit at a computer desk the rest of the time. Some well-meaning people even warned me that the search could drive me crazy. I'd grown up an Australian man, in a loving family. Fate had delivered me from dire straits into a comfortable existence – perhaps I needed to accept that the past was past and to move on.

I realise now that I was also a little scared and defensive of my memories – I'd lived with them for so long, and clung to them so tightly, that I wanted very passionately to preserve them and the kernel of hope they contained. If I went back and searched, and failed to find anything, would that mean I really did have to draw a line under the past and move on? If I could find no trace of my home and family, how would I keep holding on to their memory? Going back without certainty might ruin the little I had.

With the trail cool, I completed my course and moved back to Hobart in 2009, and found a bar job to support myself. Despite the diploma in my back pocket, it only took a few weeks for me to realise I'd lost interest in the hospitality industry. I'd had an inkling this was the case while still in Canberra, but I had wanted to complete the qualification, at least.

We all reach a point as young adults when we wonder what

we should be doing with ourselves – at least, which direction to point ourselves in. Beyond the means to get by, we need to think about what's most important to us in our lives. Not surprisingly, I discovered that for me the answer was family. Perhaps being away from Hobart for a while had strengthened this feeling. And my renewed interest in my past had prompted me to think about my relationship with my family in Hobart. It occurred to me that the Brierley family business might give me an opportunity to draw aspects of my life together, and I was excited when my parents agreed it was a good idea.

Mum and Dad own a business selling industrial hoses and fittings, valves and pumps, which Dad manages. In a remarkable coincidence, Dad started the business the day I arrived from India – he left my granddad in the brand-new office to answer any calls when he set off to Melbourne with Mum to meet me.

Joining the business meant working with Dad every day, and I quickly realised I'd made the right choice. Working with him was inspirational. I think some of his determination, work ethic and focus on success rubbed off on me. He certainly kept me busy, but I think it brought us closer. Mantosh later took the same path, so now we're all involved and working together.

At the same time, I threw myself into a new relationship, and my girlfriend and I moved in together. The move back to Hobart and all that followed reminded me that tracing my roots was not the most important thing in my life, overriding all else. I understand that may sound strange to some people. Adoptees, whether or not they ever knew their birth parents, often describe the constant, gnawing feeling of there being something missing: without a connection, or at least the knowledge of where they are from, they feel incomplete. I didn't feel that. I never forgot my Indian mother and family – and I never will – but being separated from them didn't create a block that somehow prevented me from pursuing a full and happy life. I'd learned quickly, as a matter of survival, that I needed to take opportunities as they came – if they came – and to look forward. Part of that was gratefully accepting the life I was granted through my adoption. So I tried to concentrate again on the life I had.

8

THE SEARCH

Of all people, I should have known that life takes many unexpected twists and turns. But things can still take me completely by surprise, and though I might have become better than some at coping with new circumstances – changes of career, of location, even of fortune – emotional changes can hit me as hard as they do anyone else. Perhaps even a little harder.

Working with Dad and learning to be a salesman was great – I do it to this day – but my relationship with my girlfriend proved tempestuous and we went through a difficult breakup. Although I was the one to end it, I found myself bereft and full of regret. I moved back into my parents' home and went through a dark period of conflicting emotions: rejection, disappointment, bitterness, loneliness and a sense of failure. I sometimes didn't make it to work, or made careless errors. My parents wondered when I'd pull myself back together to be the positive, forward-looking man into which they thought I'd developed.

I was lucky to have made good friends over the years. A fortuitous meeting with Byron, a guy I'd known in my bar and nightclub days, ended with him suggesting I move into a spare room at his place for a while. He had become a doctor and he introduced me to a new crowd. His kindness and the fresh faces I met really helped pick me up. If family has been the most important thing in my life, friends have not been far behind.

Byron was always going out and enjoying himself, and I liked to join him from time to time, but I was also glad to spend some time alone at home. Although I was much less depressed, I was still thinking about the breakup and wondering how to think of myself as myself, rather than part of a couple. And although I don't think my childhood made this process any easier or harder, it got me thinking about my life in India again, in earnest.

Byron had broadband internet access at home and I had a new, fast laptop. Even in the periods of my life when I hadn't felt that retracing my past was imperative, I'd never forgotten about it or ruled it out completely. In this new phase of my life, I had a fuller connection with my parents through the family business, and even felt I was giving back to them a little. That gave me the security to face the emotional risks of the search again. Yes, there was a lot to lose – each failure to find my home chipped away at the certainty of my memories – but there was also so much to gain. I wondered whether I might be avoiding the search, and also if the confidence I'd had that it wasn't affecting my ability to get on the front foot in the rest of my life was perhaps overstated. At the very least, wasn't this just a failure to buckle down, like my teenage drifting? And what if, by the slimmest of chances, I managed to find it? How could I pass up the chance of discovering where I was from, and maybe even finding my mother?

I decided that resuming the search – in a low-key way – would be part of regaining a positive outlook on life. Maybe the past could help shape the future.

It didn't start out as an obsession.

If Byron wasn't home, I might spend a couple of hours musing over the various 'B' towns again. Or I might make a casual sweep down the east coast, to see what was there. I even checked out a Birampur in Uttar Pradesh, near Delhi, in the central north of India, but that was a ridiculously long way from Kolkata and I couldn't have travelled that far in twelve or so hours. It turned out it doesn't even have a train station.

These occasional forays showed the folly of searching by town, particularly when I wasn't sure about the names. If I was going to do this, I needed to be strategic and methodical about it.

I went over what I knew. I came from a place where Muslims and Hindus lived in close proximity, and where Hindi was spoken. Those things were true of most of India. I recalled all those warm nights outside, under the stars, which at least suggested it wouldn't be in the colder regions of the far north. I hadn't lived by the sea, although I couldn't rule out that I'd lived near it. And I hadn't lived in the mountains. My home town had a railway station – India was riddled with train lines, but they didn't run through every village and town.

Then there was the opinion of the Indians at college that I looked like someone from the east, perhaps around West Bengal. I had my doubts – tucked in the eastern part of the country next to Bangladesh, the region took in some of the Himalayas, which wasn't right, and part of the Ganges Delta, which looked much too lush and fertile to be my home. But as these were people who had firsthand experience of India, it seemed silly to dismiss their hunch.

I also thought I could remember enough landmark features to recognise my home town if I came across it, or to at least narrow the field. I knew the bridge over the river where we played as kids and the nearby dam wall that restricted the river's flow below it. I knew how to get from the train station to our house, and I knew the layout of the station.

The other station I thought I remembered quite well was the 'B' one, where I'd boarded the train. But although I'd been there quite a few times with my brothers, they'd never let me leave it, so I knew nothing of the town outside the station – all I'd ever seen beyond the exit was a sort of small ring road for horse carts and cars and a road beyond it that led into the town. But still, there were a couple of distinguishing features. I remembered the station building and that it only had a couple of tracks, over the other side of which was a big water tank on a tower. There was also a pedestrian overpass across the tracks. And just before the train pulled into town from the direction of my home, it crossed a small gorge.

So I had some vague thoughts on likely regions, and some ways of identifying Ginestlay and the 'B' place if I found them. Now I needed a better search method. I realised that the place names themselves had been a distraction, or were at least not the right place to start. Instead, I thought about the end of the journey. I knew that train lines linked the 'B' place with Kolkata. Logic dictated, then, that if I followed all the train lines out of Kolkata I would eventually find my starting point. And from there, my home town was itself up the line, not far away. I might even come upon home first, depending on how the lines linked up. But it was an intimidating prospect – there were many, many train lines from the national hub of Kolkata's Howrah Station, and my train might have zigzagged across any of the lines of the spider's web. It was unlikely to be a simple, straight route.

Still, even with the possibility of some winding, irregular paths out of Howrah, there was also a limit to how far I could have been transported in the timeframe. I'd spent, I thought, a long time on the train – somewhere between twelve and fifteen hours. If I made some calculations, I could narrow the search field, ruling out places too far away.

Why hadn't I thought of it with this clarity before? Maybe I had been too overwhelmed by the scale of the problem to think straight, too consumed by what I didn't know to focus on what I did. But as it dawned on me that I could turn this into a painstaking, deliberate task that simply required dedication, something clicked inside. If all it took were time and patience to find home, with the aid of Google Earth's god's-eye view, I would do it. Seeing it almost as much an intellectual challenge as an emotional quest, I threw myself into solving it.

First, I worked on the search zone. How fast could India's diesel trains travel and would that have changed much since the Eighties? I thought my Indian friends from college might be able to make a guess, especially Amreen, whose father worked in the railways, so I got in touch with them. The general consensus was around seventy or eighty kilometres an hour. That seemed like a good start. Figuring I had been trapped on the train for around twelve to fifteen hours, overnight, I calculated how many kilometres I might have travelled in that time, which I put at around a thousand.

So the place I was looking for was a thousand kilometres along a train line out of Howrah Station. On Google Earth you can draw lines on the map at precise distances, so I made a circular boundary line of a thousand kilometres around Kolkata and saved it for my searches. That meant as well as West Bengal, my search field included the states of Jharkhand, Chhattisgarh and nearly half of the central state of Madhya Pradesh to the west, Orissa to the south, Bihar and a third of Uttar Pradesh to the north, and most of the north-eastern spur of India, which encircles Bangladesh. (I knew I wasn't from Bangladesh, as I'd have spoken Bengali, not Hindi, but it was confirmed when I discovered that a rail connection between the two countries had only been established a few years earlier.)

It was a staggering amount of territory, covering some 962 300 square kilometres, over a quarter of India's huge landmass. Within its bounds, lived 345 million people, and although I tried to keep my emotions out of the exercise, I couldn't help

ଛଅ ବର୍ଷର ବାଳକ

ସାରୁ

ଏ ଘିଟକ୍ ବୁହୁପୁରର । ଏହା ବିଷୟରେ
ଯଦି କେହି ଜାଣ୍ଥିଥିବ ସ୍ୱୟାଙ୍କି ନିମ୍ନ
ଠିକଣାରେ ସୋଗାଯୋଗ କରନ୍ତୁ ।
Indian Society for Sponsorship
and Adoption
1 KYD Street, Calcutta.
S/2675

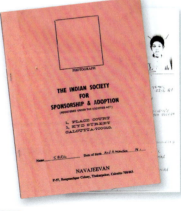

THE INDIAN SOCIETY
FOR
SPONSORSHIP & ADOPTION
(REGISTERED UNDER THE SOCIETIES ACT)

1. PLACE COURT
1. KYD STREET
CALCUTTA-700010.

Name SARU   Date of Birth Ab A/B Months   N...

NAVAJEEVAN
P-37, Rangamatigar Colony, Thakurpukur, Calcutta-700 063

After being picked up off the streets of Kolkata in 1987, I spent two months at the Nava Jeevan orphanage, run by the Indian Society for Sponsorship and Adoption (ISSA). I'm in the red T-shirt (above, left), and with my friend Asra standing beside me on the caged front porch (left). ISSA ran lost notices in newspapers (top, right), unaware my home was much farther away than where they were trying.

The photo book prepared by my new parents, the Brierleys, which I was shown at Nava Jeevan to familiarise myself with them and my new home.

FOR SAROO,
'NAVA JEEVAN'
P67, RANGANATHPUR COLONY
THAKURPUKUR, CALCUTTA

THIS PLANE WILL BRING
YOU TO AUSTRALIA

THIS IS THE HOUSE
THAT WILL BE OUR HOME
AND HOW YOUR FATHER
WILL WELCOME YOU

THIS IS THE CITY
WHERE WE LIVE —

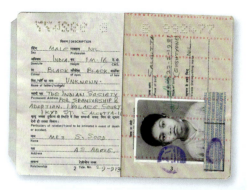

With a passport featuring an invented birthday of 22 May 1981, I left for Australia with other adoptees and official escorts, including ISSA's Saroj Sood, sitting with Asra and me on her lap. It was my first experience of the eye-opening luxury of hotels.

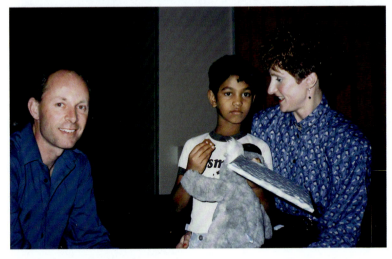

I arrived in Melbourne's Tullamarine Airport in my Tasmania T-shirt and proceeded with the escorts and other children to a VIP room, where our new parents were waiting. Mum and Dad welcomed me with a book and a koala bear. I'm still holding the remains of the chocolate bar we were given on the plane – my first word to my new parents was 'Cadbury'.

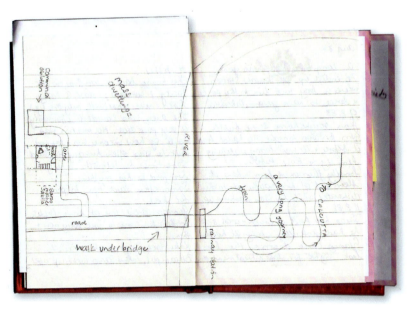

The first maps in my life – the wall map of India I grew up with in my room (seen here as it was prepared for my arrival), and the map of my home town my mother drew with me in her notebook, when at age seven I first told her the story of how I became lost.

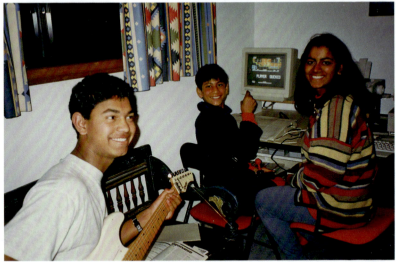

I had a happy life growing up in Hobart with my new family, which soon included my younger adopted brother, Mantosh. Above, he sits at the computer next to my friend and fellow Nava Jeevan adoptee, Asra, who occasionally visited from Victoria. Like many teenagers, I had rock star ambitions.

I didn't know the name of my childhood home town. But several years at the computer, searching with Google Earth, led to my incredible discoveries: first, Burhanpur Railway Station (above) – with its familiar water tower – from which I accidentally boarded the train that took me across the country; and then, up the line, the familiar layout of my home town itself (left).

From the satellite view of my search, to returning to India to retrace my steps on the ground: the dam by the rail bridge on the southern outskirts of my home town (opposite, top left); the park fountain, the rail underpass and the railway station (opposite); and the now-abandoned home in which I grew up, in the town's poor neighbourhood (above). Today, I dwarf the front door.

My mother, Kamla, and I were reunited after twenty-six years, at her modest dwelling (opposite, bottom) just around the corner from where we used to live. She had remained in the neighbourhood in the hope I might one day return.

Reuniting with my family was an overwhelming experience. My older brother, Kallu, and younger sister, Shekila, returned home to meet me, although tragically I would discover we couldn't be joined by my oldest brother, Guddu.

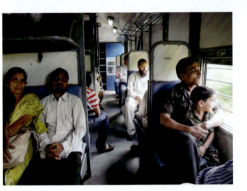

The train carriage I was trapped on was something like the one above and left – although in those days, the benches on second-class carriages were wooden and not cushioned. I will never be exactly certain of the route I was taken on across India from Burhanpur to Kolkata, but I made the journey again, as an adult with a first-class ticket (top).

In Kolkata, I found Saroj Sood (seated far left) in the same ISSA office from which she'd arranged my adoption a quarter of a century ago. My ISSA file notes: 'We consulted Saru if he would like us to look for a new family for him, and to this he agreed readily.' In the next room (above, right), new orphans napped on floor mats.

It was all too easy to see how a small child was ignored inside the huge and busy Howrah Station (top). Above and left are the imposing walls and iron gates of the Liluah juvenile home, where I was originally sent after being picked up off the streets. Now a home for women and girls only, I wasn't permitted to take photographs inside.

© Nathan Harrison

In my first weeks on the streets, I never strayed far from the distinctive red block of Howrah Station, seen from Howrah Bridge (top). The bridge is a monumental structure, which loomed over me when I survived weeks living on or around the banks of the Hooghly River.

My two families, which make me feel doubly blessed. (Top) Mum and Dad (John and Sue Brierley) and my brother Mantosh. (Bottom) Rear, from left: my brother Kallu and his wife Nasim, their daughter Norin, my mother Kamla and sister Shekila. Front, from left: Shekila's son Ayan, and Kallu's sons Shail and Sameer.

but wonder if it could be possible to find the four members of my family among them.

Even though my calculations were reliant on guesswork and were therefore very rough, and even though that still presented me with a huge field within which to search, it felt like I was narrowing things down. Rather than randomly throwing the haystack around to find the needle, I could concentrate on picking through a manageable portion, and set it aside if it proved empty.

The train lines within the search zone wouldn't all simply stretch out to the edge in a straight radius, of course – there would be a lot of twists, turns and junctions, as they wound around and travelled much more than a thousand kilometres before they reached the boundary edge. So I planned to work outwards from Kolkata, the only point of the journey I was certain about.

The first time I zoomed in on Howrah Station, looking at the rows of ridged grey platform roofs and all the tracks spilling out of it like the fraying end of a rope, I was taken straight back to being five. I was about to embark on a high-tech version of what I'd done in my first week there, randomly taking trains out to see if they went back home.

I took a deep breath, chose a train line and started scrolling along it.

*

Progress was going to be slow. Even with broadband, my laptop had to render the image, which took time – it started a little pixelated then resolved into an aerial photograph. I was looking for landmarks I recognised, and paid particular attention to the stations, as they were the places I remembered most vividly.

When I first zoomed out to see how far I'd gone along the track, I was amazed at how little progress hours of scrolling and studying had brought me. But rather than being frustrated and impatient, I found that I had enormous confidence that I would find what I was looking for as long as I was thorough. That gave me a great sense of calm as I resumed my search. In fact, it was quickly compelling and I returned to it several nights a week. Before I turned in, I'd mark how far I'd gone on a track and save the search, then resume from that point at the next opportunity.

I would come across goods yards, overpasses and underpasses, bridges over rivers and junctions. Sometimes I skipped along a bit, but then nervously went back to repeat a section, reminding myself that if I wasn't methodical I could never be sure I'd looked everywhere. I didn't jump ahead to look for stations, in case I missed a small one – I followed the tracks so I could check out anything that came along. And if I found myself reaching the edge of the boundary I'd devised, I'd go back along the train line to a previous junction, and then head off in another direction.

I remember one night early on, following a line north, I came to a river crossing not far outside a town. I caught my breath as I zoomed in closer. There wasn't any dam wall, but maybe it had since been taken away? I quickly dragged the cursor to roll the image along. Did the countryside look right? It was quite green, but there were a lot of farms on the outskirts of my town. I watched as the town unpixelated before my eyes. It was quite small. Too small, surely. But with a child's perspective . . . And there was a high pedestrian overpass across the tracks near the station! But what were the large blank areas dotted around the town? Three lakes, four or five even, within the tiny village's bounds – and it was suddenly obvious that this wasn't the place. You didn't clear whole neighbourhoods to put in lakes. And of course, many, many stations were likely to have overpasses, and many towns would be situated near life-giving rivers, which the tracks would have to cross. How many times would I wonder if all the landmarks aligned only to be left with tired, sore eyes and the realisation that I was mistaken again?

Weeks and then months passed with me spending hours at a time every couple of nights on the laptop. Byron made sure I spent other nights out in the real world, so I didn't become an internet hermit. I covered the countryside of West Bengal and Jharkhand in these early stages, without finding anything familiar, but at least it meant that much of the immediate vicinity of Kolkata could be ruled out, despite the hunch of my Indian friends – I'd come from further away.

Some months later, I was lucky enough to meet someone with whom I started a new relationship, which made the search less of a priority for a while. Lisa and I had an unsettled start together, with a couple of breakups and reunions, which meant there was a similar inconsistency in the periods I spent looking on the internet, before we finally settled into the lasting relationship we have today.

I didn't know how a girlfriend would take to the time-consuming quest of her partner staring at maps on a laptop. But Lisa understood the growing importance the search had for me, and was patient and supportive. She was as amazed at anyone about my past, and wanted me to find the answers I was looking for. We moved into a small flat together in 2010. I thought of the nights I spent there on the laptop as being a pastime, like playing computer games. But Lisa says that even then, with our relationship in full swing, I was obsessive. Looking back, I can see that this is true.

After all the years of my story being in my thoughts and dreams, I felt I was closing in on the reality. I decided this time I wasn't going to listen to anybody who said 'It might be time to move on' or 'It's just not possible to find your home town in all of India like this.' Lisa never said those things, and with her support, I became even more determined to succeed.

I didn't tell many people what I was doing, not even my parents. I was worried they might misunderstand my intentions: they might think that the intensity of my search revealed an unhappiness with the life they'd given me, or the way they'd raised me. I also didn't want them to think that I was wasting time. So even as it took up more and more of my life, I kept it to myself. I finished work with Dad at 5 p.m. and by 5.30 I would be back home and on the laptop, slowly advancing along train tracks and studying the towns they led to. This went on for months – it had been over a year since I started. But I reasoned that even if it took years, even decades, you could eventually sift completely through a haystack – the needle would have to show up if you persisted.

I slowly eliminated whole areas of India. I traced all the connections within the north-eastern states without finding anything familiar, and I was confident I could rule out Orissa too. Determined to be thorough, no matter how long it took, I started following lines further out than my original thousand-kilometre zone. South beyond Orissa, I eliminated Andhra Pradesh, a further 500 kilometres down the east coast. Jharkhand and Bihar didn't offer up anything promising either, and as I wound up into Uttar Pradesh, I thought I'd keep going to cover most of the state. In fact, the states eventually replaced my zone boundary as a way of marking my progress. Ruling out areas state by state provided a series of goals that spurred me on.

Unless I had something pressing to do for work, or some other unbreakable commitment, I was on the laptop seven nights a week. I went out with Lisa sometimes, of course, but the moment we got home I was back on the computer. Sometimes I caught her looking at me strangely, as though she thought I might be a bit crazy. She'd say, 'You're at it again!' but I would reply, 'I have to . . . I'm really sorry!' I think Lisa knew she simply had to let me exhaust myself of the interest. I became distant during that time, but although Lisa would have been within her rights to feel alone in this still-new relationship, we worked through it. And perhaps to some extent sharing something so fundamental to me strengthened our connection – and that came through when we sometimes talked about what it all meant to me. It wasn't always easy for me to articulate, especially as I was trying to keep a lid on my expectations, trying to convince myself it was a fascinating exercise, not a deeply meaningful personal quest. Talking to Lisa sometimes revealed the underlying importance of the search to me: that I was looking for my home to provide closure, to understand my past and perhaps myself better as a result, in the hope that I might somehow reconnect with my Indian family so they would know what had happened to me. Lisa understood all this and didn't resent it, even if there were times when she wanted to ban me from staring at the screen, for my own sake.

Lisa sometimes said her greatest fear was that if I found what I was looking for and decided to go back to India, what would happen if the place was somehow wrong or if I didn't find my family there? Would I return to Hobart and simply start again, obsessively searching online? I couldn't answer that. I couldn't let myself think about failing.

If anything, I became more intense about my search as 2010 drew to a close, and the speeds of our newly acquired ADSL 2+ broadband connection made it quicker to refresh the images and zoom in and out. But I still had to take it slowly – if I rushed I'd leave myself open to wondering later if I'd missed anything. And I had to try not to bend my memories to fit what I was looking at.

By early 2011, I was concentrating more on areas of India's centre, in Chhattisgarh and Madhya Pradesh. I spent months poring over them; relentless, methodical.

Of course, there were times when I doubted the wisdom, and even the sanity, of what I was doing. Night after night, with the day's last reserves of energy and willpower, I sat staring at railway lines, searching for places I might recognise in my five-year-old mind. It was a repetitive, forensic exercise, and sometimes it started to feel claustrophobic, as if I was trapped and looking out at the world through a small window, unable to be break free of my course, in a mind-twisting echo of my childhood ordeal.

And then, one night in March, in just such a mood, at around one in the morning, I took a wild dive into the haystack in frustration, and it changed everything.

9

FINDING HOME

As always, on 31 March 2011 I had come home from work, grabbed my laptop, opened Google Earth and settled in for a session on the sofa, stopping only briefly for dinner when Lisa got home. I was examining the central west at this time, so I picked up there, 'travelling' a train line near my former search zone boundary. Even with broadband, it was still slow going. I continued for what I thought was ages, looking at a few stations, but as usual, when I zoomed out, I found I'd only covered a tiny area. The countryside looked a bit green for my dusty old town, I thought, but I knew by now that India's countryside changed appearance regularly as you moved across it.

After a few hours, I had followed a line to a junction and I took a break, checking Facebook for a while, before rubbing my eyes, stretching my back and returning to my task.

Before zooming back in, I idly flicked the map along to get a quick picture of where the westerly line out of the junction headed, and watched hills, forests and rivers sweep by, a seemingly endless terrain of reasonably similar features. I was distracted by a large river that fed into what looked like a massive, deep blue lake called Nal Damayanti Sagar, apparently, which was surrounded by some lush country and had mountains to its north. For a while I enjoyed this little exploration, indulgently unrelated to my search, like a recreational hike of grand proportions. It was getting late, after all, and I'd turn in soon.

There didn't seem to be any train lines in this part of the country, which might have been why it was relaxing to look at. But once I'd noticed that, I found myself almost subconsciously looking for one. There were villages and towns dotted around here and there, and I wondered how the people travelled without rail – perhaps they didn't get around much. And further west, still no tracks! Then, as the countryside flattened out into farmlands, I finally came across a little blue symbol denoting a train station. I was so attuned to looking for them, I was somehow relieved to find it, and I checked out the tiny wayside station, just a few buildings to the side of a reasonably major train line with several tracks. Out of habit, I started tracing the route as it wound south-west. I quickly came across another station, a bit bigger, again with a platform on only one side of the tracks but some areas of the township on either side. That explained the overpass, and was that . . . was that a water tower just nearby? Holding my breath, I zoomed in for a closer look. Sure enough, it was a municipal water tank just across from the platform, and not far from a large pedestrian overpass spanning the railway line. I scrolled over to the town side and saw something incredible – a horseshoe-shaped road around a square immediately outside the station. The ring road I used to be able to see from the platform. Might it be? I zoomed out, discovering that the train line skimmed the north-west of a really large town. I clicked on the blue train station symbol to reveal its name – it was called Burhanpur.

My heart nearly stopped. *Burhanpur!*

I didn't recognise the town, but then, I'd never been in it – I'd never left the platform. I zoomed back in and re-examined the ring road, the water tower, the overpass, and they were all positioned where I remembered them. That meant, not far away, just up the line, I should find my home town, Ginestlay.

Almost afraid to do so, I dragged the cursor to pull the image north along the train line. When I saw that the track crossed a gorge just on the edge of the built-up area, I was flooded with adrenalin – I remembered in a flash that the train I took with my brothers travelled on a small bridge over a gorge like that, before pulling in to the station. I pushed on more urgently, east then north-east, zooming in moments over seventy kilometres of green farms, some forested hills and small rivers. Then I passed across some dry flat land broken up by a patchwork of irrigated farmland and the occasional small village, before I hit a bridge over a substantial river and I could see the town's outskirts ahead. The river's flow was significantly reduced below the bridge by dam walls on either side. If this was the right place, this was the river I used to play in, and there should be a bigger concrete dam wall to my right a little further from the bridge.

And there it was, clearly visible as if on a sunny day, which it must have been when the satellite passed overhead and took the picture.

I sat staring at the screen for what seemed like an eternity. What I was looking at matched the picture in my head exactly. I couldn't think straight, frozen with excitement and terrified to go on.

Finally I forced myself to take the next step, slowly, nervously. I tried to calm myself so I didn't make any rash judgements. If I really was looking at Ginestlay for the first time in twenty-four years, then I should be able to follow the path I remembered from the river back to the train station, only a short way up ahead. I began to drag the cursor again, slowly rolling the map to trace the course of the path, which wound gently alongside a tributary stream, left and right, around a field, under a street overpass and then . . . the station. I clicked on the blue symbol and the name came up on the screen: Khandwa Railway Station.

The name meant nothing to me.

My stomach knotted. How could this be? Things had looked so right all the way from Burhanpur, which surely must be the 'B' town I had tried to remember. But if the bridge and the river were correct, where was Ginestlay? I tried not to despair. I had spent a lot of time in and around our local train station as a boy, so I checked off what I remembered – the three platforms, the covered pedestrian overpass that connected them, an underpass road beneath the tracks at the northern end. But it wasn't so much the existence of these reasonably common features but their position in relation to each other that would identify the place. It all checked out. I also remembered a huge fountain in a park near the underpass and went looking. And sure enough, it was a little indistinct, but I thought I detected its familiar circular shape in a centre clearing, surrounded by trees.

From here, I knew the route to where home should be. This was why I'd gone over and over it in my head since I was a little boy, so that I never forgot it. I followed the road up from the fountain and along the route of the underpass, and then the streets and alleys I had walked as a child – the way I used to imagine myself walking when I lay in bed in Hobart at night, trying to project myself home to let my mother know I was okay – and, before I realised I'd gone far enough, I was looking down at the neighbourhood I knew as a boy. I was sure of it.

Still, nothing like 'Ginestlay' came up on the map. It was the strangest feeling, and one that I became familiar with over the next year or so – part of me knew but part of me doubted. I was sure this was the right place, but for all this time I'd also been sure of the name 'Ginestlay'. 'Khandwa' rang no bells whatsoever. Maybe Ginestlay was a part of Khandwa, a suburb. That seemed possible. I looked through the maze of alleys where we lived, and although the image wasn't as clear as I would get when I looked at where I lived in Hobart, I was sure I could see the little rectangular roof of my childhood home. Of course, I'd never seen the place from above, but the building was the right shape and where it ought to be. I hovered over the streets for a while, astonished, trying to take it all in, before I couldn't contain my excitement any longer.

I called out to Lisa, 'I've found my home town! You've gotta come and see this!' It was only then that I realised it was the middle of the night – I'd been at the computer for over seven hours non-stop, except for dinner.

Lisa poked her head around the corner, yawning, in her nightie. It took her a moment to wake up properly, but even half-asleep she could see I was excited. 'Are you sure?' she asked. 'This is it, this is it!' I replied. In that moment I was convinced. 'This is my home town!'

It had taken eight months of intense searching, and was nearly five years since I'd first downloaded Google Earth.

Lisa grinned and hugged me tightly. 'That's so great! You did it, Saroo!'

After a sleepless night, I went to see Dad in his office at work. For him, the news was going to come out of the blue, and I knew he might take a little convincing. I tried to rehearse what I was going to say in my head, hoping to lend it some gravity, but in the end, all I managed was to put on a stern face as I said, 'Dad, I think I've found my home town.'

He stopped working on his computer. 'Really? On a *map*?' I could tell he was sceptical. 'You're sure?'

It was a natural response to the sheer improbability of the discovery. What had happened? Had I suddenly remembered where I came from after all these years? I told him I was indeed sure, and how I'd found it. He remained doubtful, partly to protect me from the possibility I was wrong. Caution was understandable, but I needed him to know that I was convinced and wanted him to be too.

In retrospect, one of the reasons I was so keen for Dad to

believe me was that telling him was the start of the journey back to India for me. Lisa was, of course, always in on my search and my hopes for it, but telling Dad made the discovery real, and also the need to do something about it. I didn't have firm plans about what to do next, but sharing the news made me realise that this was the start, not the end, of a journey. From that moment, it was clear that this was a life-changing discovery, for all of us, even if I found out nothing more.

Telling Mum was another step. She knew I had some interest in finding my Indian home and that I looked for clues on the internet, but not that I'd been actively searching. It was she that I was particularly anxious about upsetting. Mum had such a dedicated belief in adoption and the family it had made, I was worried about how my news would affect her.

So that night we gathered at the family home, each of us slightly on edge. For my part, I was eager to show them the Google Earth images that had convinced me I'd found my home town. They responded tentatively. The idea that I'd used a bird's-eye view to search one of the most populated countries on earth, looking for landmarks I remembered from when I was five, and that I'd actually found what I was looking for, was incredible, or at the very least a great surprise. I showed them the walled dam on the southern edge of Khandwa, the train lines and the underpass I walked through to get to the station, just as I had described to Mum when I was little.

At the back of our minds, I think we all wondered what this discovery would mean for the future. I wondered whether they'd always thought this day would come, and feared their son would be reclaimed by India and perhaps lost to them.

We had a slightly muted celebratory dinner with lots of questions in our minds.

When I arrived home afterwards, I was full of nervy energy and went straight back to my computer. Maybe I had been carried away – maybe there were other ways of confirming what I already knew. I turned to another tool that hadn't been around when I started my search – Facebook. I searched for 'Khandwa', and up came a group called 'Khandwa: My Home Town'. I sent a message to the group administrator:

> can anyone help me, i think I'm from Khandwa. i haven't seen or been back to the place for 24 years. Just wondering if there is a big fountain near the cinema?

The fountain was the most distinct landmark I could think of. The park where it was located was a busy meeting place, and the circular fountain had a statue on a plinth in its centre, of a wise man sitting cross-legged. I never knew who he was supposed to be. But some of the town's dreadlocked holy men – who I now know as sadhus – bathed in its cool waters and forbade anyone else from doing so. I remembered once gashing my leg on a barbed wire fence running away from them, after my brothers and I crept in on a really hot day. There were probably better ways to try to identify the place – who knew what might have been demolished since my time there? – but I hadn't really imagined what I'd do when I reached this stage. It now seems absurd, but I suppose I thought I'd find a town labelled 'Ginestlay' and that would be that; I'd know I'd found home. But nothing else had worked out as I thought it would – this town was well outside my search boundary, and after all my careful planning and methodical efforts I'd found it by accident. It seemed almost fitting that it should turn up this way – my destiny appeared to be riddled with close calls, chance episodes and wonderful, blessed luck.

I went to bed for another restless night.

Mum and Dad's caution proved well founded. When I woke the next day, I opened my computer first thing and saw that I'd received a response to my query about the fountain on the Khandwa Facebook page:

well we cant tell u exactly . . . there is a garden near

cinema but the fountain is not that much big . . . the
cinema is closed for years . . . we will try to update some
pics . . . hope u will recollect some thing . . .

It was deflating, and I cursed myself for getting carried away
and telling everyone too early. Why hadn't I waited to get word
back from the place itself? But I tried to stay calm. Although this
wasn't the confirmation I'd been hoping for, it certainly wasn't
a complete dismissal either. I thanked the administrator and
headed off to work in a mental fog. It was hard to concentrate
as maps and memories swirled around my mind. Could it all be
wishful thinking? Had I been wasting my time?

Later that day, or the next, Mum told me she had looked at
the map we'd drawn together in her notebook when I was six,
and the configuration of the bridge, the river and the train station weren't quite what I'd shown her on Google Earth – but
was that because I had the wrong place, or because I'd had trouble drawing an accurate map as a six-year-old? She'd also pulled
out the wall map I used to have in my bedroom – she kept everything to do with my brother's and my upbringing – and had
been surprised to find that it had both Burhanpur and Khandwa
marked on it. To her, they seemed so far away from Kolkata
that she wondered whether it was possible I'd travelled that distance. It was almost all the way across the country.

The first thing that hit me was that my home had been marked on the map above my desk the whole time, if I'd only known where to look. How many times had I looked at all those names, not knowing their secrets? I don't remember if I ever noticed Burhanpur among the several similar names on the map when I was younger; if I had, I'd obviously written it off, probably as being too far from Kolkata. And that was the second thing – it *was* much further than I had thought possible. Was it too far? Did the trains go much faster than I'd allowed for? Or had I been on the train for longer than I thought?

Two surreal days passed. I was stuck between maps and memories. The things I'd always been so certain about were dissolving in the face of what I'd found. Was what I'd always feared actually happening? Would the search erode what I thought I knew and leave me with nothing? My parents, Lisa and I didn't talk much more about my breakthrough, and I wondered whether they were being overly protective or waiting for me to produce some solid evidence. It took me all that time, waiting for a second reply from the Khandwa group, to think to ask them the obvious question:

Can anyone tell me, the name of the town or suburb on the top right hand side of Khandwa? I think it starts with G . . . not sure how you spell it, but i think it goes like this

(Ginestlay)? The town is Muslim one side and Hindus on the other which was 24 years ago but might be different now.

It took another day to get an answer. But when the answer came it was heartstopping:

Ganesh Talai

That was as close to my childhood mispronunciation as you could hope for.

In my excitement, I called Mum and Dad immediately to tell them that now there could be no doubt. They remained worried but conceded that it all lined up. I had found Burhanpur and Khandwa and now, vitally, I had found Ganesh Talai, the area where I'd lived, where my Indian family might still be living, wondering what became of me.

In the immediate aftermath of my discovery, I wasn't sure what to do – it was overwhelming. On the one hand, I was so excited I'd succeeded it was hard to think about anything else. But on the other, underneath these feelings was a faint nervous uncertainty, which meant for the time being I kept the news between Lisa, my family and me. What if I was wrong? What if I was stirring everybody up on the basis of a mistake? What if I was making a fool of myself? I kept revisiting the streets of Khandwa on my laptop, probing them for more revelations and confirmations, almost paralysed by the prospect of the truth. It was like when Mantosh and I were kids, too scared to go to India on the family trip. I was anxious, and the anxiety expressed itself as doubt.

From the moment I found the place, I tried to keep a lid on my expectations. I tried to convince myself my family couldn't possibly be there after all this time. How old would my mother be by now, I wondered. I wasn't sure, but life expectancy probably wasn't that great, and she'd lived a hard life as a labourer. Was my sister, Shekila, okay? And Kallu? What had happened to Guddu that night in Burhanpur? Did he blame himself for my getting lost? Would any of them recognise me if we met again? Would I recognise them? How could you possibly find four people in India, even if you knew where they lived a quarter of a century ago? Surely it was impossible.

My mind pinged back and forth between hope and denial, trying to find some way to settle with these new possibilities.

There was, of course, only one way to be sure. I wouldn't know that this was the right place for certain without going there. I would know it if I saw it. And then, if I was completely convinced, I told myself, I would be happy just to take off my shoes and feel the earth beneath my feet, and remember the times when I used to walk the streets and paths. I couldn't let myself think further than that, about anyone who might still be living there.

I knew my parents would worry about my going to India. I was much older than the child they'd planned to take, but that didn't mean the same feelings that had made them cancel the last trip weren't still there to be stirred up in the adult. And if it was the wrong place, what would that do to me? Would I stay there and search for the right one? Would I despair entirely?

I spent some time researching Khandwa and got to know it as an adult from half a world away. It's a small regional city of less than a quarter of a million people, in the majority-Hindu state of Madhya Pradesh – a quiet area well known for its cotton, wheat and soybean farming, as well as a major hydro power plant. My family was too poor to be involved in any of that, so all of this was news to me. Like most Indian cities, it's got a long history and a list of Hindu saints attached to it, and it can boast a list of Bollywood stars who grew up there. Although it's not on the tourist trail, it is on a significant rail junction, where the major east–west line between Mumbai and Kolkata meets another trunk route running from Delhi down to Goa and Kochi. That explains why Khandwa's station is much larger than the one at Burhanpur, although the towns are about the same size.

I watched the few clips of the town on YouTube, but it was hard to tell much from these images. Some footage showed the underpass near the railway station, apparently known as Teen Pulia, and the pedestrian overpass across the tracks, which appeared to have been extended over all three platforms. It still looked like home.

Some weeks passed this way before I summoned the courage to raise with Mum and Dad the question of going to India. Even then I edged round to it – I asked them what they would do in my situation. They said it was obvious: I had to go. Who wouldn't want to visit to make sure? Lisa felt the same way. And, of course, they all wanted to come with me.

I was relieved, and touched, but I needed to go alone.

I felt strongly about this for a number of reasons. Partly, I still worried about the possibility of being mistaken – what if we ended up standing in some back street, with Mum and Dad and Lisa staring at me as I was forced to admit I didn't know where we were? I didn't want to make a big scene, either – a group of us descending on Ganesh Talai would probably draw lots of attention, and who knew what stresses that might cause?

This was quite a big issue for me, in fact. I had realised I could probably track down the phone number for the local police or the hospital in Ganesh Talai and call ahead to ask them about my family or search for my medical records. I could provide my family's names, at least, and make some enquiries. It's not a big neighbourhood, and everyone knew everyone. But I feared that word would get out very quickly and chancers would start appearing, making false claims. Some might well like the idea of a Western, comparatively well-off prodigal son, and it wouldn't be surprising if a few potential 'mothers' turned up at the station ready to claim their long-lost boy. By the time I got there, I might have made it harder to find the real people I was looking for. Without any pre-announcements or entourage, I ought to be able to slip in relatively unnoticed and make my own judgements.

Moreover, I didn't know what to expect – possibly even dangerous situations in such an unpredictable country – and I didn't want to have to worry about everyone else, or to be distracted by them. Alone, I would just have the facts of my situation, and my own response to it, to deal with.

Maybe ultimately my reasoning was even simpler than that: this was my journey and thus far I'd made it by myself, from the trains to the late nights on the internet – it just felt right that I complete it alone.

Thankfully, Lisa said she understood. But my parents were more insistent. Dad promised that they would keep out of the way and let me do what I needed to do on my own. Or, perhaps just he could come, for support and to help with any problems? He could stay in the hotel, but at least he'd be on hand. 'I won't slow you down,' he said. Although these were kind and well-meaning offers, I'd made up my mind.

Still, it was eleven months after I first identified Ganesh Talai that I eventually got on the plane. Apart from my childhood flight to Australia, it was my first major trip anywhere, and in addition to the usual travel stuff, there were more than the usual administrative questions to resolve – even the matter of citizenship. When I had arrived from India my passport showed that I was an Indian citizen. But it was not entirely accurate: it also stated that I was born in Calcutta, which, of course, was incorrect, but the Indian authorities had needed to put something in. Now I was an Australian citizen, and my Indian citizenship had expired but it hadn't been officially renounced. Little bureaucratic details like these all took time to get through.

But underneath all this, the truth is I was putting things off. I tried not to show it – and didn't even really acknowledge it to myself – but I was extremely anxious about the trip. Not only were there the questions of whether I'd got the right place and whether there'd be anyone there to reunite with; I also had to face up to some bad memories with the prospect of returning to India. I wondered how I'd handle it.

Still, I booked my ticket, refused offers of company, and tried to prepare myself. Support came from unusual quarters. When I went to the medical clinic for the necessary vaccinations, my doctor asked the reason for my travel. Although I had generally kept my story to myself and close friends, now that I felt I'd found my home I was less guarded about it, and for some reason I told him a little, and then a lot, about what was taking me to India. He was stunned and thanked me for sharing the incredible details. As I returned for follow-up vaccinations, others at the surgery learned my story too, and I received a lot of attention from wellwishers. It was nice to feel this other team was on my side in the weeks leading up to my departure, and it helped keep me in good spirits.

When the day finally came, Mum, Lisa and I had a final cup of coffee together at the airport and went through the possible scenarios that awaited me once more. They told me to try to take it as it came, and not to get overwrought with what I wanted to happen. So perhaps I hadn't done such a great job of disguising my anxiety after all. Then Mum handed me an A4 sheet of photos she had scanned, showing me as a little boy. It had been twenty-five years since I'd been seen in India – even my own family might need help recognising me. It was an extremely smart parting gift – I couldn't believe that with all my fretful preparations I hadn't thought of it myself, but that probably says a lot about my state of mind.

Even then I lingered with final goodbyes and was the last to board the plane. Mum looked at me nervously and that triggered my own worries once more. Was I doing the right thing? Did I need to find out about the past, when I had people who loved me very much right here with me now?

But of course the answer was yes, however nervous it made me. I had to find out where I was from, if I could, even if only to put it behind me. I wanted to see the place I always dreamed about, at least.

I got on the plane.

10

MEETING MY MOTHER

When I landed on 11 February 2012, in the city of Indore, the biggest city in Madhya Pradesh, my feet touched the ground in India for the first time since I left as a child. In the pre-dawn dark I felt a rush of adrenalin as the magnitude of what I was doing hit me.

India didn't exactly welcome me back. My first experiences firmly established me as a stranger – I might have come 'home', but this was a country foreign to me. My bag was missing from the luggage claim carousel. When I tried to ask an airport official where it might be, he replied in what I think was Hindi and I didn't understand a word. The official soon went to fetch someone who spoke some English. It seems a little thing, to not speak the language, but it carried extra weight for a man making an emotional journey home after years of being lost. It was like being lost all over again, unable to understand what anyone said or to make people understand me.

I made a mess of negotiating my way out of several insistent but exorbitant offers of a taxi to the hotel where I was staying the night before going on to Khandwa, and eventually found the courtesy bus. The sun blazed into life as we pulled out of the airport, and I got my first look at the pressing confusion of twenty-first century India.

At first, much of it looked like the India I had known a quarter of a century earlier. I saw black wild pigs scavenging in side streets, the same sorts of trees on street corners, and the familiar press of people everywhere. The poverty of the place was still plainly on show, but I was quickly struck by how much dirtier everything appeared from how I remembered it. I saw people relieving themselves on the roadside and rubbish strewn everywhere – I didn't remember the same things from my own neighbourhood, but maybe I'd become accustomed to the clean, open spaces of Hobart.

When I got out at the hotel, the unrelenting noise of heavy traffic and the strong smell of sulphur, from drains and sewerage, hit my senses. I realised that after such a long time Khandwa would probably seem different too. After a fitful few hours' sleep, I organised a car and driver to take me there the next day.

Khandwa was two hours' drive away, and I paid half of what the spruiking drivers at the airport had asked for to take me the few kilometres to the hotel. That reminded me that any sort of street-smarts I used to have were long gone. But perhaps you paid extra for safety: my short, skinny driver took to the roads like a maniac, even by the famously carefree standards of India, which added another shot of adrenalin to my overloaded system. The road from Indore runs through hills and valleys, but I noticed little of the scenery. We stopped occasionally for a chai and a cigarette – I rarely smoke, but my nerves demanded it – and I found myself growing more and more anxious about what awaited me in Khandwa. The death-defying trip couldn't go quickly enough.

Under a hot sun in clear skies, we approached the outskirts of town. I found I didn't recognise it at all, which gave me an instant chill. The area had a dusty grey industrial look that I didn't recall. Suddenly, I decided to go straight to the railway station, before the hotel – I was past dragging things out, and that would be the quickest and easiest way to discover whether what I had worked out on my laptop back at home in Tasmania was right. We changed direction.

The roads were narrow and traffic slowed to a crawl – it was Sunday and people were out and about everywhere. When I was little, there had been more horses and carts than autorickshaws, but now the streets were clogged with cars and motorbikes.

My mobile phone had a GPS service, which would have laid out a street map for me, but my batteries were low and I wanted my memory to be jolted into service. So I directed the driver as best I remembered the way, and, sure enough, we found the station where I expected it to be. He might have been humouring me, I guess, and already knew the way, but my spirits lifted.

The station looked a little different from how I remembered it, but I found I instantly had my bearings – from there, I knew the way to anywhere in Khandwa. I knew where I was, and I wasn't far from home.

I was elated.

At that point exhaustion overwhelmed me. I felt like a puppet with his strings cut. Nervous energy had been sustaining me since I arrived in India – and for a long while before that – and now that I felt like I was in the right place, I couldn't go any further. I asked the driver to take me to the hotel – I'd walk the streets the next day.

As the taxi crawled through those streets, I tested them against my memory. I remembered the place being green, with trees everywhere, less industrialised and polluted, and certainly with no garbage in the streets. The buildings looked much shabbier than I had pictured them. But when we drove through an underpass beneath the train tracks with barely any overhead clearance, memories of just such a claustrophobic road came flooding back. It was surely the one where I had played as a child.

At the Hotel Grand Barrack – as the name suggests, it was once a British Army barracks – I inadvertently offended my driver by offering no *baksheesh*. From being in Australia, I simply wasn't used to paying more than the agreed amount, and I walked inside the hotel before I realised my mistake. I checked in, feeling like I was carrying a culture clash around within me.

Exhausted by my discoveries, and the lengthy travel, I put my suitcase down in my hotel room, switched on the air conditioning and overhead fan, and collapsed on the bed.

But, tired as I was, I couldn't settle. Perhaps I was overwrought, but I thought, What the heck am I doing? I've been sitting on planes for an eternity, squashed in a car for two hours more . . . Get going! It was Sunday, two o'clock, I had come a long way to find my home. I grabbed my daypack and water bottle, and felt a surge of excitement.

Standing outside the hotel, I didn't know which way to go first – roads and lanes led off in every direction – so I retraced the route the car had taken. Soon I was walking on the road parallel to the railway line, striding back towards the centre of town.

Despite a certain familiarity about the streets, I couldn't

quite say that I knew precisely where I was. So much was different, I just couldn't be sure. Doubts began to creep back into my mind – after all, how different could railway stations and underpasses look in Indian towns and cities, and how many towns and cities were there? Might I have made a mistake? But my feet seemed to know the way, as though I was on automatic, and jetlag, fatigue and the surreal nature of the experience made me feel like I was observing my progress from outside myself. I was failing to take Mum's advice to remain calm and keep my expectations low. Instinct, memory, doubt and excitement were all coursing through me at once.

After a while, I came upon a small green mosque. Baba's mosque. I had forgotten all about it! It looked similar to what I now remembered – more rundown and of course smaller, but the resemblance was still reassuring. I began to feel again that I was on the right track. But I still questioned relentlessly everything I saw – Did it look like that? Was it right? Was I right?

Eventually I thought I should turn left, to head towards the centre of Ganesh Talai. I began to tremble and my pace slowed. This didn't look right at all. There were too many houses – it looked too built up. I tried to calm myself down – things change, populations grow. Of course it was more crowded. But if old buildings had been knocked down for new ones, maybe my house was gone too! That made me shudder, and I hurried on until I came to a small section of open ground that looked like a spot where I used to play.

I recognised it and yet I didn't. It was the same place, but different. Then I realised what the difference was: the town now had electricity. There were poles and wires everywhere. When I was growing up we had lit our house with candles and cooked on a wood stove or with kerosene. Now that the streets were draped with electricity cables, the whole place looked more closed in, busier – transformed.

I had worked myself up into a state, less, I suspect, about identifying the place and the buildings and more about what else might have changed. I'd deliberately not allowed myself to think about my mother and my family, and now I was approaching where they might still be. Despite my best efforts, all sorts of emotions were bubbling to the surface.

Still I put it off. I decided it was best to start by trying to find the first house my family had lived in, while we were still living in the Hindu neighbourhood.

Making my way down a street and into a narrow, twisting alleyway, I saw a woman at its end washing clothes. As I looked down the alley, memories of running around the place flowed through me. I must have been staring, because she spoke to me – a strange man in casual Western sportswear, probably rich-looking, certainly looking out of place. I think she said something like 'Can I help you?' in Hindi, but all I knew to respond with was 'No.' I turned and walked on.

After that I couldn't delay the inevitable any longer. Finally it was time to face up to the ultimate point of my journey. It only took a few minutes to walk across the few streets that once separated the Hindu and Muslim areas of the neighbourhood. My heart was in my mouth as I approached the place where I remembered the crumbling brick flat to be. And before I could think about what I was expecting, I found myself standing right in front of it.

It looked so tiny to me, but it was unmistakable.

It was also unmistakably abandoned. I stood and stared.

The rough brick walls were familiar, though the ground level was now plastered with cheap concrete and whitewashed. The doorway to the corner room was in exactly the right place – but the door itself was broken. It was the size of a window in Australia. I couldn't see much through the cracks in the door, so around the corner I peered in through the sole window, barely thirty centimetres square. I couldn't believe that my mother, sister, brothers and I – although not always at once – had occupied the tiny dark space inside. It was perhaps three metres square. The little fireplace was still there, clearly not used for some time, but the clay water tank had gone. The single shelf was hanging off its brackets. Some of the outer wall's bricks had fallen away, letting in beams of light. The cowpat and mud floor, which my mother had always kept swept clean, was now dusty from disuse.

While I looked in, a goat chewed at some hay left on a rock by the door, indifferent to my personal disaster. Although I'd told myself over and over that I couldn't expect to just fly to India and find my family safe and well in the same place after all this time, it was hard to absorb that I'd found the flat without any of them in it. Despite my best efforts, secretly I had been convinced that if I found my way back home, they'd be here waiting. I watched the goat eat, in a daze, completely hollowed out with disappointment.

I had no idea what to do next. My search was over.

As I stood there, for the first time with no plan in mind, a young Indian woman holding a baby came out of the next door. She spoke to me in Hindi and I understood she was asking if she could help me. I replied, 'I don't speak Hindi, I speak English.' I was jolted out of my slump when she said, 'I speak English, a little.' Quickly, I said, 'This house . . .' and then recited the names of my family: 'Kamla, Guddu, Kallu, Shekila, Saroo.' The woman didn't respond, so I repeated the names and pulled out the sheet of photos Mum had given me before I left. That was when she told me what I couldn't bear to hear: that no-one lived there anymore.

It was then that two men walked over to see what was

happening, and it was the second – perhaps in his mid thirties, and with good English – who looked at the photos, told me to wait, and then walked off down an alley. I didn't have much time to think about what was happening – other people had begun gathering near us, curious as to what was going on, and about the presence of a foreigner in these streets where tourists would never visit.

After a couple of minutes the man returned and said those word I'll never forget: 'Come with me. I'm going to take you to your mother.'

He said it very directly, like an official making an announcement, so bluntly that I just accepted it. I didn't absorb what he'd said until I'd begun to do as he asked and follow him down an adjacent alley. Then I got goosebumps and my head began to spin – just moments ago I'd given up twenty-five years of hoping for exactly this. Could it possibly be true that this passing stranger knew where my mother was? It seemed too unlikely and too fast. After all this time, things were moving at a bewildering pace.

After only about fifteen metres, the man stopped in front of three women who were standing outside a doorway, all of them looking in my direction. 'This is your mother,' he said. I was too stunned to ask which one – I half-wondered whether this was a prank.

Incapable of doing anything else, I looked from one to the next. The first was certainly not her. There was something familiar about the woman in the middle, and the third woman was a stranger. It was the woman in the middle.

She was slender and seemed so small, with greying hair pulled back in a bun, and wearing a bright-yellow floral dress. Despite the years, I knew the fine bone structure of her face the instant I looked back at her, and in that moment she seemed to know me too.

We looked at each other for a second longer, and I felt a sharp stab of grief that it took a mother and son so long to recognise each other, and then a rush of joy that we now had. She stepped forward, took my hands and held them, and stared into my face with utter wonderment. I was thinking clearly enough to understand that whatever turmoil I was feeling, at least I'd had some chance to prepare. For my mother, twenty-five years after losing him, her son had simply reappeared.

Before either of us had said anything to each other, my mother led me by the hand to her house. A long line of people followed, curious to see what was happening. Her house was only a hundred metres around the corner. As we walked, she seemed overcome with emotion. She said things to herself in Hindi, then looked up at me again and again, with tears of joy in her eyes. I was too overwhelmed to say anything.

Her house, another conjoined dwelling of crumbling brick, was down a dirt alley, and she bustled me inside and sat me down on her bed in the main room. She remained standing and produced a mobile phone from within the layers of her clothing. When she said, 'Kallu, Shekila . . .' I understood that she was calling my siblings. They were still here too? She spoke excitedly on the phone, screaming and laughing, and calling out, 'Sheru! Sheru!' It took me a moment to realise that my mother was saying my name. Was it possible I'd been mispronouncing my own name all this time?

The little knot of people that had assembled outside was growing rapidly, and soon there was quite a crowd. They were chatting excitedly to each other and into mobile phones – the miracle of the son returned from the dead was clearly big news, and word was being spread. The house was soon filled with boisterous, celebrating people, with more crowded in the alley outside the front door and even more gathered up on the adjoining street.

Fortunately, some of these wellwishers had a little English, and my mother and I were finally able to talk through translators. The first thing she asked me was, 'Where have you been?' It would be a little while before I could give her an expansive answer, but I provided a quick sketch of how I came to be lost in Kolkata and ended up being adopted in Australia. Not suprisingly, she was astonished.

My mother told me that the man I had spoken to in the street had come to the house she was visiting and simply said to her, 'Sheru is back.' Then he had shown her the sheet of paper with the photographs on it that Mum had given me – and which I don't even remember him taking – and said, 'This boy who is now grown into a man is nearby and asking about Kamla, which is you.' That seemed a strange thing to say, but I learned that my mother had converted to Islam many years earlier and had taken the new name Fatima. I think she will always be Kamla to me.

My mother described her reactions better than I ever could mine: she said she was 'surprised with thunder' that her boy had come back, and that the happiness in her heart was 'as deep as the sea'.

When she had seen the photos she had started shivering and ran from the house into the alley, where she was joined by the two women she had been visiting, and that was where they had been when I appeared at the top of the alleyway. She said as I walked towards her she had still been shivering, and felt cold, with 'thunder in her head' as joyful tears welled in her eyes.

I had thunder in my head, too. And after all the slowness

of travel and the quiet yet highly emotional ups and downs of walking the streets of Ganesh Talai to our old flat, now everything was happening in a mad, chaotic rush. There were people shouting and laughing everywhere, pressing in to get a look at me, a babble of Hindi I couldn't understand, and my mother smiling and crying. It was too much to comprehend.

Later, I realised that I had been just fifteen metres away from her, literally around the corner, when I turned up in front of our old home, but if that man had not come along and helped me I might have walked away. I probably would have found her in the end, after asking around more, but I'm haunted by the chance that I might not have, that we might have stood so near to each other and never known.

We were really only able to talk in fits and starts, as messages were translated, and people asked questions, and the story was repeated for the benefit of newcomers. My mother would turn to her friends, grinning widely, then simply look at me or hug me with tears on her face. Then she'd get on the phone again for a while, to spread the word.

There were a lot of questions to be answered, of course, and most of them by me. My mother had no idea what had happened to me since that night I disappeared. With so much to fill her in on, it was slow work, but luckily, after a while, we had the help of an unlikely interpreter, a woman who lived a few doors away, called Cheryl. Her father was British, her mother Indian, and she had somehow found herself living in Ganesh Talai. I was so grateful to have Cheryl's help; with it, by degrees I managed to make myself understood to my mother. Later I would be able to tell her everything, but at that first reunion I could only cut through the chaos with the basics: being trapped on a train, ending up in Calcutta, and being adopted and growing up in Australia. That I had come back after so many years was astonishing to my mother; that I'd come from somewhere as far away as Australia was incomprehensible.

Even at this first meeting, though, she told me she was grateful to my parents who had raised me in Australia, and that they had the right to call me their son because they had raised me from a child and made me the man I was today. Her only concern for me, she said, was that I should have the very best life I could. It was extremely moving to hear her say these words. She wasn't to know it, but they took me back to being a little boy at the Nava Jeevan orphanage, deciding whether to accept the Brierleys' offer of adoption. She allowed me to feel, without reservation, that I'd made the right decision. She also said she was proud of me, which is all anyone can wish to hear from their mother.

The rundown building she lived in was in some ways even more dilapidated than our abandoned home. The bricks in the front wall were crumbling, leaving obvious gaps. In the front room of about two by three metres, where she slept on the single bed on which she had me seated, two pieces of corrugated iron came down from the roof to a junction, obviously to channel rainwater into a bowl in the small adjacent bathroom, with its squat toilet and tub of water for washing. It disturbed me to see that the way it was built also meant that rain would just blow inside. There was a slightly larger room at the back, serving as a kitchen. But though it was far too small for all the curious people who were trying to get inside, her home was larger than our old place, and at least it had a terrazzo floor rather than compacted dirt. It was in shocking condition, but in the context of Ganesh Talai, it represented a step up, and I knew she would have had to work hard for that. I learned from others that she was too old to carry stones on her head on building sites anymore, and now worked as a house cleaner. Despite the hardness of her life, she told me she was happy.

People kept arriving over the next couple of hours, crowding around the barred window and the doorway, excitedly chatting and being filled in on the gossip. My mother held court for many groups of visitors, sitting next to me and holding my face or hugging me while she talked, or leaping up to take a phone call.

Finally, two special guests were ushered inside, in quick

succession – my brother, Kallu, and sister, Shekila. When Shekila arrived, with her husband and two sons, our mother was holding me and crying, and my sister burst into tears as I stood to embrace her. Kallu then arrived alone on a motorbike, and was stunned to lay eyes on me – I knew how he felt. We instantly recognised each other, but each saw his brother as an adult for the first time. Neither of my siblings had had any cause to learn English, so this was another reunion of tears, smiles and speechless wonder, before some simple communication with Cheryl's assistance. It was bittersweet to be so close to my family and yet still cut off in this fundamental way.

But where was Guddu? Of all the stories I wanted to hear, his was top of the list. What had happened that night in Burhanpur? Was it something he thought about often? Above all, I wanted him to know that I didn't blame him for anything – I was sure it was an accident, and now I'd finally found my way back.

That's when I was told the hardest news I heard that day – indeed, the hardest news I've ever heard. When I asked my mother about him, she replied sadly, 'He is no longer.'

Guddu hadn't come home either after that night I was lost. My mother found out a few weeks later that he had died in a train accident. She had lost two sons on the same night. I couldn't imagine how she had borne it.

If there was one thing more I could have wished for from

that visit, it was to see Guddu again, even if only once. It was because I'd missed him so much that I made him take me to Burhanpur. To hear that he had died was devastating.

Later, I learned more about that evening and what my mother thought had happened to us both. At first, she was a little annoyed that I'd gone off with Guddu, because I was needed to look after Shekila. But the India I began life in was not like Australia, where a child missing for an hour can cause alarm – my mother was herself often gone for days, and even young children might be in and out of the house unsupervised. So initially she wasn't too concerned. But after a week had passed, she began to worry. It wasn't unusual for Guddu to be away for weeks, but it was irresponsible of him to keep me away for this long. Kallu hadn't seen us on his travels and didn't know whether we'd been around Burhanpur, and my mother started to fear the worst. She had Kallu ask around Khandwa and Burhanpur if anyone had seen us, but they heard nothing.

A few weeks, possibly a month, after our disappearance, a policeman came to the house. More worried about me, being the youngest and least capable, my mother thought he had come with news of where I was, but he hadn't – he had come about Guddu. He said that Guddu had died in a railway accident, and showed her a photo of his body. Guddu was found by the tracks about a kilometre outside Burhanpur, and the policeman was there to ask her to formally identify him. I asked if she had been sure it was him, and she nodded slowly. It was still a very painful subject for her, so I got the rest of the details from Kallu. Guddu, just fourteen, had somehow fallen from a moving train, and either went under a wheel or struck something fixed by the side of the track. Half of one of his arms had been severed and he had lost one of his eyes – an unimaginably horrific thing for a mother to have to look at.

I wanted to visit Guddu's grave, but my family told me that wasn't possible – houses had been built over the graveyard he was in. The builders hadn't even moved the remains of the dead before they began construction. The owners or developers didn't want to know, or didn't care. It wasn't easy to hear. I felt as if my brother had been taken from me, just as I had been taken from him – disappeared without trace – and in a corner of my mind I understood a little more of what my family must have felt about my vanishing. We didn't even have any photographs of Guddu, as we could never afford family portraits. He had been part of us, as we had been part of him, and now all that remained of Guddu was our memories.

I wasn't sure that my family entirely understood why I was so upset about not having a grave to sit by. For them it was long in the past, but for me his death had happened that very day. Not being able to grieve for him properly was something

I felt I really missed after I returned to Australia. The last thing he had said to me on that platform in Burhanpur was that he would be back. Perhaps he'd never returned; perhaps he'd come back to find me gone. Either way, I'd hoped to be able to be reunited with him. Now I'll never know what happened that night – some of our mysteries will never be solved.

My family feared I had suffered the same fate, or something even worse. They weren't even sure whether I was alive or dead. I felt for Kallu particularly: he lost two brothers and suddenly became the eldest male, which carried responsibilities in our community. He would have been seen as equally responsible for the family's welfare with my mother, a huge weight on his young shoulders.

I also learned a little about my father. He was still alive, but no longer lived in Khandwa – he'd moved with his second family to Bhopal, the capital of Madhya Pradhesh, a couple of hundred kilometres to the north, the city that was made famous by a chemical disaster at the Union Carbide plant in the early Eighties. The family still hated him for abandoning us, so my curiosity about him would have to wait.

Amid all the chaos and celebration that first day, Cheryl mentioned to me that some of the people there were asking my mother how she was sure I was her son. Wasn't it possible that I was an imposter, or that we were both mistaken, swept away in events because we so wanted them to be true? My mother answered that a mother knows her child anywhere – she'd had no doubt I was who I said I was from the first moment she saw me. But there was one way to be completely sure. She held my head in her hands and tilted it, looking for the scar above my eye from when I fell in the street, running away from a dog. There it was, on the right side, just above the brow. She pointed to it and smiled – I was her son.

My mother's house was full of wellwishers late into the evening. Eventually I had to go – I was completely drained, and my head and heart were full to bursting. It took a long while to say goodbye to everyone, even without many words in common – there were lots of long looks and hugs. I suppose at the back of everyone's minds was the question of whether, after I walked out of the door this time, I'd come back. I promised that I would, the next day. My mother finally let me go, and watched as I climbed behind Kallu on his motorbike and sped off. We couldn't talk, but I thanked him as I got off at the Grand Barrack and he left for the hour's ride back to Burhanpur, where, ironically, he now lived – the town I'd spent so long trying to find.

Back in my room, I thought about how my life had completely changed since I left it, just that afternoon. I had found my family. I was no longer an orphan. And the search that had meant so much to me for so long was over. I wondered what I was going to do now.

I thought a lot about Guddu. It was hard to imagine what might have happened to him. Guddu was so confident getting on and off trains, having worked on them for so long, that I found it hard to believe he just fell. Could there be another explanation? Perhaps he had returned to discover me gone and went looking for me. There were kids my brothers had run-ins with from time to time – maybe he'd got it into his head that they had done something to me and started a fight? The worst possibility was that he might have felt guilty about leaving me alone, and in his panic to find me had taken risks or been preoccupied, and fallen.

He might have assumed I'd gone home, but he never went back to check, so it was hard not to think that if I hadn't boarded the train that night, Guddu might have returned as planned and he'd still be alive now. Intellectually, I knew I couldn't accept responsibility for his fate, but it was a dark thought that was hard to shake. And although I usually felt there was an answer for everything, that you just needed to work at a problem until you solved it, this time I understood that I would have to accept I could never know the truth of what had happened to my brother.

Before getting into bed, I sent a text to Mum and Dad at home in Hobart:

> The questions I wanted answered have been answered. There are no more dead ends. My family is true and genuine, as we are in Australia. My mother has thanked you, mum and dad, for bringing me up. My brother and sister and mum understand that you and dad are my family, and they don't want to intervene in any way. They are happy just knowing that I'm alive, and that's all they want. I hope you know that you guys are first with me, which will never change. Love you.

Not surprisingly, it was hard to sleep.

11

RECONNECTION

Kallu picked me up on his motorbike early the next morning and took me back to our mother's house. She greeted me almost as enthusiastically as she had the day before; perhaps she really hadn't believed that I would come back.

Kallu had already delivered his wife, son and daughter to the house before coming for me, and he presented them to me – incredibly, all four had made the trip from Burhanpur on the motorbike. I had been delighted the day before to discover I was an uncle, to Shekila's two sons, and I loved meeting my niece and third nephew.

It was briefly quiet as we had tea, smiling at each other, but before long it was all on again, exchanging stories with help from Cheryl and other translators, and greeting endless visitors – and that was how it was to be for the next four days. Shekila soon joined us with her husband and children, having again made the two-hour journey from her home in Harda, a hundred kilometres to the north-east.

My family inevitably asked me about my wife and kids. It surprised them that I didn't have any. I suppose by this age I'd have a family too if I'd grown up in India. But they seemed pleased to hear that I had a girlfriend, at least, although I wasn't sure my mother understood the concept.

By that second day, the local news media had heard about the lost boy who had suddenly re-materialised as a man in the streets of Ganesh Talai. They were soon joined by the national media, who arrived bristling with TV cameras. Their questioning – mostly through translators – was relentless, and as I told my story over and over again, it began to feel as though it had happened to someone else.

The media interest came as a genuine surprise. It hadn't crossed my mind that my return would cause such a fuss, and I wasn't remotely ready for it. It made an emotionally demanding situation even more so, but I found something wonderful in it too. There are more than a billion people in India, and there are kids roaming the streets with no-one to care for them. It can seem a chaotic, even harsh, place. Yet here in Ganesh Talai – in fact, around the whole country – people could get wildly excited because just one of those lost children had managed to reconnect with their family after an incredibly long time apart.

As even more people came flocking to see me, the gathering turned into a public celebration, with music, and people dancing in the streets. My return seemed to inspire and energise the neighbourhood, as though it was evidence that the hard luck of life did not have to rule you. Sometimes, miracles happen.

We seem to be a family that holds emotions in until they build up such pressure that we have no choice but to release them. When we had some time to ourselves, we all wept a lot, from happiness but also from the sadness of the time we'd lost – I was now thirty, Kallu thirty-three and Shekila twenty-seven. I had last seen Shekila as a tiny infant whom I'd had to keep watch over, and now she had two beautiful children of her own.

I remembered something and grabbed a bit of charcoal from the fireplace, showing her. She laughed. When she was only one or two years old, I would sometimes find her eating charcoal, perhaps out of hunger, her face blackened by it. She became addicted to it. (It had a terrible effect on her digestive system, and we had to take her to a woman who had some special knowledge about how to fix her. Luckily, it seemed to cause her no lasting damage.) The fact that we could laugh about it now showed how far we had come from those days.

Shekila and Kallu were lucky enough to have gone to school. With Guddu and me gone, our mother had just been able to afford to send them. Shekila had become a schoolteacher, able to speak and write Hindi and Urdu (but not English). Shekila told me that when she got the call from our mother the day before, she hadn't believed it – she'd thought it might be someone pulling a scam, or playing a joke. But my mother's conviction, and especially her description of the sheet of photos of me as a kid, brought her round. She'd thanked God for the miracle and quickly got on a train to join us. When she had laid eyes on me again, she had been 'lost in time', taken back to the days when I looked after her. She had known it was me straightaway.

Kallu had also done well for himself. He was now a factory manager, with a supplementary income as a school bus driver. So in one generation, my family's occupations went from stone-carrying labourer to teacher and manager. It seems a bittersweet result of the family's loss that the remaining children had managed to lift themselves out of poverty. But life hadn't been easy for Kallu – I was deeply saddened to hear that I'd been right about his life after Guddu and I disappeared. The burden of being the only man in the house had weighed on him heavily. Although he had also been sent to school after my disappearance, he had cut his schooling short in order to learn to drive, so he could get better work to try to support Shekila and our mother. The pain of loss had never left him, and eventually caused him to leave not only Ganesh Talai but Khandwa altogether, and move to Burhanpur. He told me that he'd even questioned his Hindu faith at times, but had eventually felt that the gods would 'do justice' one day, by having me come back. My return affected him deeply – perhaps it would mean that some of the wounds he had carried for so long could begin to heal, and the burdens be shared.

We talked more about the difficult times my family had endured after my disappearance – Shekila even admitted to being scared about sending her little kids to school, in case one day they didn't come back – but there was laughter too, of course. One thing that left me bemused was the discovery that I was christened Sheru, Hindi for 'lion'. I'd mispronounced my name ever since I became lost – and now I'd forever be Saroo.

I found that being in Ganesh Talai brought back a lot of memories about my life there, and talking with my family brought back even more. Many of them I was too young at the time to understand. The things I learned that day, and in the couple of days that followed, helped me to fill in some of the gaps in the picture of my early life – a life that's ordinary for millions of small-town Indians. It also helped me understand the life my birth mother had led; her resilience in the face of its harshness made me admire her even more.

My mother's family was of the Rajput warrior caste, and her father was a policeman. She was named Kamla after the Hindu goddess of Creation. I remembered her as having been beautiful, and I still found her so now, despite the passage of so many backbreaking and often heartbreaking years.

My father was shorter than her, broad-chested, with a square face, and even as a young man his hair was flecked with grey. He always dressed completely in white, in the Muslim custom, and he worked as a building contractor. He was twenty-four and my mother eighteen when they married.

I've now learnt much more about why I rarely saw my father. When I was around three, Guddu nine and Kallu six, and with my mother pregnant with Shekila, my father announced he had taken another wife – which he was permitted to do as a Muslim – and was leaving us to live with her. My mother had apparently known nothing of my father's intention to marry again until he announced that he'd done so – a rude shock. My father had met his new wife at one of his building sites, where she was a labourer, hefting bricks and stones and transporting them around on trays on her head. My mother would still see my father at times, where he lived, on the town's outskirts. His second wife was very jealous of her and would see her off, and my mother was convinced it was she who prevented my father from seeing us. I certainly can't remember him visiting us at home.

My mother decided against seeking a divorce, although she could have done so under Islamic law, having been abandoned by her husband. She remained married to my father, even though he no longer lived with or supported her.

She was deeply disturbed by all that had happened and describes that terrible time as like a hurricane tearing through her life. Sometimes she was so disorientated that she didn't know where the sky ended and the ground began. She wished to die – she even contemplated having us all take poison, or lie down on the nearby railway line to be killed by the first passing train.

It was then that she decided to move us to the Muslim part of Ganesh Talai, to the flat that now lay unoccupied. She felt her Hindu family wouldn't take her back in, but the Muslim community seemed supportive of her despite her circumstances. I suspect she also felt their more prosperous neighbourhood would be a better environment for her children to grow up in. I now found that the religious segregation I remembered had since been relaxed, and there were no longer clearly distinguished areas.

Despite the move, my mother didn't formally convert to

Islam until after my disappearance, although she didn't veil her face, as some of her friends who visited did. I don't remember having any religious instruction as a child, although I did occasionally visit the local shrine kept by Baba. But I do remember simply being told one day that I wasn't to play with my friends anymore because they were Hindus. I had to find new – Muslim – friends.

The biggest impact Islam had on my upbringing wasn't pleasant – circumcision. I don't know why I had to endure it even though we weren't converts – perhaps my mother thought it wise to go along with some of the local area's customs to keep the peace, or maybe she was told it was a requirement of our living there. For whatever reason, it was done without anaesthetic, so it's unsurprisingly one of my clearest and earliest memories.

I was playing outside with some other kids when a boy came up and told me I was needed at home. When I got there, I found a number of people were gathered, including Baba. He told me that something important was going to happen, and my mother told me not to worry, everything would be all right. Then several men I recognised from the neighbourhood ushered me into the larger upstairs room of our building. There was a large clay pot in the middle of the room and they told me to take my shorts off and sit down on it. Two of them took hold of my arms, and another stood behind me to support my head with his hand.

The remaining two men held my body down where I sat on top of the clay pot. I had no idea what was going on, but I managed to stay calm – until another man arrived with a razor blade in his hand. I cried out, but they held me fast as the man deftly sliced. It was very painful, but over in seconds. He bandaged me up and my mother nursed me on a bed. A few minutes later, Kallu went into the upstairs room and the same thing happened to him, but not Guddu. Perhaps he'd already had it done.

That night the neighbourhood held a party, with feasting and singing, but Kallu and I could only sit on our rooftop, listening. We weren't allowed to go out for several days, during which time we were forced to fast and wore only a shirt with no trousers, while we recovered.

Without my father's financial support, my mother was forced to seek work. Soon after the birth of Shekila, she went off to labour on building sites, like my father's new wife. Fortunately, she was a strong woman and able to do the heavy work involved. The pay was negligible (although standard for rural labour in India at that time) – a handful of rupees for carrying heavy rocks and stones on her head in the hot sun from morning until dusk. She worked six days a week for something like a dollar and thirty cents. Guddu went to work too, and his first long shift washing dishes in a restaurant earned him less than half a rupee.

Begging for food in the Muslim neighbourhood provided a more varied diet than we'd had before – we occasionally got to eat meat, such as goat and chicken. I also remember we ate special foods during a festival or party, for a marriage or other celebration, and these seemed to come around fairly regularly. There was often a festival of some sort going on, and that meant we all had some fun and free food – and lots of it.

For clothing, we wore hand-me-downs from neighbours. Luckily, with the warm climate, we didn't need much. Simple cotton clothing sufficed. Education was out of the question. The school I used to hang around, watching the lucky students come and go, was Saint Joseph's Convent School, which Khandwa children still attend.

Being the eldest, Guddu had felt responsible for our survival, and he had been always looking for extra jobs to bring in a little more money. He had been told it was possible to make money hawking things on the railway station platform, so he started selling toothbrush-and-paste kits to travellers. That landed him in jail, under some interpretation of child labour laws. He was known to local police – as were Kallu and I, and many young boys in our neighbourhood – as a chancer, maybe a petty thief. For example, we had worked out how to cut holes in bales of rice or chickpeas stacked at the station for the cargo trains, to collect some food for our table. Generally, we'd get away, or get a clip over the ear, and weren't considered great menaces to society. But for some reason, although Guddu was arrested that time under laws designed to protect him, they kept him in jail.

After a few days, a local policeman told my mother where he was. She took us all to the juvenile prison, an imposing complex of buildings, and pleaded with the officers until Guddu was released. I have no idea what she said, but it would have been clear she wasn't leaving without her son.

Our mother was raising us alone – our father had abandoned us completely. My family told me that when he did live with us, he could be violent, taking his frustrations out on us. Of course, we were helpless – a lone woman and four small children – against an angry man. He wanted to be rid of us, at the insistence of his new wife, and even tried to force us to leave Khandwa altogether. But my mother had no money to leave, nowhere to live and no other way to survive. Her small web of support didn't extend beyond Ganesh Talai. Eventually, my father and his wife quit the neighbourhood themselves and moved to a village on the outskirts of Khandwa, which improved things for us a bit.

I was too young to understand the separation of my parents. My father simply wasn't around. On a few occasions, I found I had been given rubber thongs and was told he'd bought new shoes for all of us.

The only memory I have of seeing my father was when I was four and we all had to go to his house to visit his new baby. It was quite an expedition. My mother got us up and dressed and we walked into the centre of Khandwa in the terrible heat to catch the bus. I kept a particular eye on Shekila, who was exhausted by the walk and the heat. The bus journey was only a couple of hours, but with the walking and waiting, the journey took all day. There was another hour's walk at the other end, and it was night by the time we reached the village. We spent the night huddled together in the entranceway of a house owned by some people my mother knew – they had no room inside to offer, but the nights were hot and it wasn't unpleasant. At least we were off the streets. Only the next morning, after we had shared a little bread and milk, did I find out my mother wasn't coming with us – she was not permitted. So we four children were escorted up the road by a mutual acquaintance of our parents to our father's place.

Despite all this – or perhaps through being oblivious to it – I was very happy to see my father when he greeted us at the door. We went inside and saw his new wife and met their baby. It seemed to me his wife was kind to us – she cooked us a nice dinner and we stayed the night there. But in the middle of the night I was shaken awake by Guddu: he said he and Kallu were sneaking out and asked if I wanted to come along. All I wanted to do was sleep. When I woke again it was to hear my father answering a loud knocking at the front door. A man had seen my brothers running from the village into the open country beyond. The man was worried they could be attacked by wild tigers.

I later learned that Guddu and Kallu had attempted to run away that night – they were upset by what was happening in our family, and wanted to get away from our father and his other wife. Fortunately, they were found later that morning, safe and sound.

But one problem morphed into another: the same morning, standing in the street, I saw my father approaching and realised that he was chasing after my mother, with a couple of people following behind him. Not far from me, she suddenly stopped and spun on her heel to face him, and they argued and shouted angrily. Quickly they were joined by other people, on both sides. I understand now that their perhaps personal argument tapped into the tension between Hindus and Muslims at the time and quickly turned into a confrontation, with the Hindus lining up with my mother, facing the Muslims lined up with my father. Tempers rose very high, and many insults were exchanged. We children gravitated towards our mother, wondering what would happen with all the shouting and jostling. Then, shockingly, my father hurled a small rock that hit my mother on the head. I was right next to her when it struck her and she fell to her knees, her head bleeding. Luckily, though, this act of violence seemed to shock the crowds too, cooling tempers rather than exciting them. As we tended to my mother, the crowd on both sides started to drift away.

A Hindu family found the room to take us in for a few days while my mother rested. They told us later that a police officer had taken my father away and locked him up in the cells at the village police station for a day or two.

This episode stayed with me as an example of my mother's courage, in turning to face down her pursuers, but also of the vulnerability of the poor in India. Really, it was just luck that the crowds backed off. My mother – and perhaps her children – could easily have been killed.

Still, perhaps because I'd been away for so long, I was open to the idea of seeing my father again. It might be hard to imagine why, with so few memories of him and none very favourable. But he is a part of my identity, part of the story of my life. And perhaps sometimes families ought to offer forgiveness to people who did the wrong thing in the past. However, with him some distance away, and my not knowing if he would want to see me anyway, I decided it wouldn't happen during this trip. I didn't mention these thoughts to anyone at the time, and as it was something I'd only want to do with their blessing, I knew

I'd have to raise the subject carefully, when I had become reacquainted with them.

As I spent more time with my family and reconnected with the place I'd been born, I thought about the word everyone kept using, including me – 'home'. Was that where I was, finally?

I didn't know. After being lost, I'd been lucky enough to be adopted by a loving family, and not only lived somewhere else, but had become someone else from the person I might have been had I stayed in India. I didn't just live in Australia; I thought of myself as an Australian. I had a family home with the Brierleys and had made my own home in Hobart with my girlfriend Lisa. I knew I belonged, and was loved, in those places.

But finding Khandwa and my Indian family also felt like coming home. Something about being in the place just felt right. I was loved here too, and belonged, in a way I'd not thought much about beforehand and found hard to explain. This was where I'd spent my first years, where my blood was.

So when it was time for me to return to Hobart – a time that came around far too quickly – I felt the wrench of leaving deeply. I promised my mother, sister and brother, and their young families, that I would be back soon. I had come to see that I'd had two homes, each with their own emotional connections, even if they were thousands of kilometres apart. This journey, which I'd embarked upon to resolve questions about who I was, wasn't finished. I had some answers – lots of answers – but I also had a lot more questions, and maybe didn't have real answers, but they kept on being asked nevertheless. One thing was obvious: the trip between India and Australia – between my homes – was one I was destined to make many times.

12

REACHING OUT

While in India, I had received an excited text of congratulations from my friend Asra, who had heard the news of my family reunion through our parents. Our families had remained close since our arrival in Melbourne all those years ago. When I got back to Hobart I called her to share some of the joy of my experiences, mindful that, sadly, she cannot make the same journey, as she had been orphaned by the death of her Indian parents. Asra was very happy for me and asked what I was going to do now I'd succeeded in reconnecting with my past. It had been such a whirlwind of revelations and emotions since I returned to Khandwa, I didn't know what to say.

I hadn't imagined anything much beyond finding my home and, maybe, my mother. I suppose I'd thought of it as the end of the story, but it was truly more like a new beginning. I now had two families, and I had to work out how I fitted in to both of them – across the world and across cultures.

My parents and Lisa were relieved to have me back. Even though we'd spoken on the phone every day I was in India, they were worried there were things I wasn't telling them. At first, they thought I might disappear again. Then Lisa kept worrying about my safety – I was in one of the poorer parts of a strange country, and who knew what to expect? I only fully realised when I got back how nerve-racking it had been for them.

That was soon forgotten, though, as everyone was anxious to hear about me meeting my family. They knew the main facts, of course, and now wanted all the details – what stories we had told each other, what the others had remembered of my childhood that I didn't, whether I wanted to return.

They seemed to be trying to work out whether I still wanted to be here, or was thinking of moving to India. I reassured them as much as I could that although the experience had changed me in important ways, I was still the same Saroo. In reality, it took me a while to feel like my old self again, and to look at Hobart through my old eyes, rather than those of a poor Indian person.

But one thing about me had changed, and it quickly became apparent: I was now someone with a story to tell, and lots of people wanted to hear it. The Hobart newspaper *The Mercury* contacted me soon after I returned. A reporter had got wind of the story somehow and I agreed to be interviewed about it. That opened the floodgates. After *The Age* in Melbourne and the *Sydney Morning Herald* came the international media.

We weren't prepared for my newfound celebrity – perhaps nobody can be. We sometimes had the phone ringing in the middle of the night as reporters called up from all over the world. I realised I needed help dealing with this attention and got a manager. Soon, book publishers and film producers were calling with offers. It was surreal. I'm a salesman for industrial pipes, hoses and fittings; I'm not someone who looks for the limelight – I only looked for my home town and family! While I enjoyed telling my story, it had never occurred to me that I'd be the sort of person who had a manager, and had to schedule media engagements. Fortunately, Lisa and my parents were very supportive and gave me all the time I needed. And even though it was exhausting to go over my story again and again with the media, I thought I had a kind of duty to do it, because it might help people – what had happened to me was remarkable and might offer hope to others who wanted to find their lost family but thought it impossible. Perhaps people in different situations could also be inspired by my experience of grasping opportunities, no matter how daunting, and never giving up.

During this time, I stayed in touch with my Indian family

with online video conferencing, which they could access with a computer at a friend's house. Or, at least, they could partly access it – they didn't have a video camera at their end so I couldn't see them, but they could see me, and we could talk, either in our stilted way or through a translator. I decided I'd have to set my mother up so that we could stay in touch and see each other from across the world. Now that the family had finally been reunited, I wanted to play a proper part in it, building our connection, and helping to look after my mother and my niece and nephews.

There were still many things I wanted to know and I hoped they would become clearer when I returned to India for my second visit. It was almost winter, although the weather was still warm and the air was a choking smog. With weather like this, the sky is an orange-grey and it doesn't change much as day turns to night.

I was heading to Khandwa in time for the end of Diwali, the Hindu 'Festival of Lights'. As with much Indian culture, I had forgotten nearly everything about it, but Indians love festive occasions so I knew it would be colourful. Diwali is a celebration of all things good and a rejection of evil. Lakshmi, the goddess of prosperity, is invoked and praised, and families display their wealth before her image in their household shrine, and give thanks for it. There's feasting and gift-giving, and traditionally little oil lamps are lit throughout people's homes, and buildings are covered with coloured lights, like in Australia during Christmas. There are also a lot of firecrackers, and I heard loud bangs all day, as people let them off to drive away evil spirits. At night, the sky was lit up by fireworks.

I arrived as evening was settling, reaching the narrow streets of the old part of town as it was in the full swing of the festivities. My mother had told me I was always welcome to stay with her, but I knew she understood that I lived as a Westerner now, and needed space and amenities her tiny flat couldn't provide. I thanked her for her generosity, but told her it would be better for me to make use of the hotel, which wasn't far away, and visit her daily. So I had dropped my bags at the Hotel Grand Barrack and then had the taxi driver take me to join her and my family in Ganesh Talai.

We drove through the railway underpass, the streets alive with people out shopping, and the driver dropped me off in the square near Ganesh Talai's temple and mosque – located tolerantly close to each other. I set off on foot down the alleys of my childhood, feeling a little more at home.

I had been trying to learn Hindi before I returned and I'd made some progress, but once I was in any sort of conversation,

I was all at sea. (I've heard there is a man on YouTube who boasts to teach Hindi in three days and I might one day give him a try – but I've a feeling there's no shortcut.)

I was greeted with warmth and joy from my mother. She had been very accepting of my 'other life', especially considering she had no real knowledge of Australia – other than through cricket. There had been a one-day series on between Australia, India and Sri Lanka at the time of my first visit, and my mother said that after I'd left, whenever she saw cricket telecasts from Australia she would reach out to the screen, hoping I was in the part of the crowd her fingers touched. Shekila and Kallu had travelled from their homes again to be there too. I was welcomed back into the family without reserve.

My mother insisted that, as her guests, we all sat in her plastic chairs while she sat on the floor at my feet. We didn't need too many words to communicate how pleased we were to see each other, but it was terrific when Cheryl arrived to translate for us once more.

Still, talking was slow work. Often I would ask a one-sentence question, and then everyone else would talk among themselves in Hindi for what felt like five minutes before I got an answer back, usually just another single sentence. I guess Cheryl had to edit. She was very generous, a patient woman with a keen sense of humour, which was just as well, as my mother, Shekila and Kallu all liked to joke around: it seems to be a family trait.

I met a woman called Swarnima who spoke perfect English and was so interested in my life story that she had offered to come and translate for us for a while. I made arrangements to pay Swarnima for her time, but she returned the money. In fact, I learned from her parents that she'd been upset that I had seen it as a professional relationship and not an offer of friend-ship. I was overwhelmed by her generous sprit, and we became good friends.

Over several days, we all spent afternoons in my mother's front room, talking – and drinking chai and eating – usually in the company of relatives and friends, with Swarnima translating over the noise of the rusty little fan in the old bamboo rafters of the roof. My mother seemed to fear that I was still undernour-ished, even though twenty-six years of an Australian diet had certainly fixed that, and kept trying to feed me.

The taste of her goat curries is one of my strongest memories from my early years in Ganesh Talai. I have eaten goat curry in many places, from wayside cafes to upmarket restaurants, but I can honestly say I've never tasted any comparable with the one my mother cooks over her little stove in the back room of her home. There is something about the balance of spices and the consistency of the meat – if goat is not cooked correctly, the fibres stick on your teeth – that she has down to perfection.

I know that sounds like a typical proud son's praise – but it's also the truth! I've cooked a lot of goat curries at home in Tasmania following the recipe I got from my mother on my first visit, but hers is always the best.

We talked a lot during this visit about how the family had never entirely written off the idea that I might come back. My mother had seen Guddu's body and therefore knew for sure he had died, but she told me they didn't mourn me as they did him because they couldn't quite believe I was dead. They had received some curious assurance in this belief. My mother never stopped praying for my return, and visited many priests and religious leaders in the community, asking for help and guidance. They always told her I was healthy and happy in good circumstances, and, amazingly, if asked where I was they would point a finger to the south and say, 'He's in that direction.'

They did what they could to find me. It was an impossible task, of course – they had no idea where I could have gone. But my mother spent every spare bit of money on looking for me – paying people to search, and even occasionally travelling herself around the area, from town to town, asking for any word. Kallu said they had talked a lot with police in Burhanpur and Khandwa – and that he had worked extra time to earn more money to help fund the family's searches. They never learned anything.

They couldn't have had 'child missing' posters printed even if they could have raised the money, because there weren't any photos of me. Praying was all they had left to do.

I began to realise that just as my search for my mother had in some ways shaped my life, her faith that I was alive had shaped hers. She couldn't search, but she did the next best thing: she stayed still. In conversation, I had wondered why she was still living in Ganesh Talai, when she could have gone to Burhanpur and lived with Kallu and his wife. She replied that she had wanted to stay near the house she had been living in when I disappeared, so that if I ever came back, I could find her. I was knocked over by the thought. It's true that if she'd moved further away, I would have had no chance of tracking them down. The strength of her belief that I hadn't died seems to me now the one of the most incredible aspects of the whole story.

I've experienced so many coincidences and strange happenings that I've just learned to accept them – even to be grateful for them. Kallu and Shekila told me they had always treasured their memories of us playing together and taking baths together as children – all the fun and mischief of our earliest years. Right from the start in Hobart, I used to imagine them in India, each night before I went to sleep. I, like them, would think about the good times we had shared together, and tried to send my mother messages that I was all right and thinking of her and the family, hoping that they were still alive and well. Could a strong emotional bond create a kind of telepathic connection? It sounds far-fetched, but I've been through so much that defies reason that I can't entirely dismiss the idea. It seems to me that somehow the message was received.

Finally, my mother told me that one day she was praying to Allah for blessings on her family when an image of me appeared in her mind. The very next day, I walked back into Ganesh Talai, and into her life.

This visit, we also talked about how our lives were changing, since my return. My mother told me that because of the publicity from the news reports, many families would wish for their daughters to marry me, but she wanted me to know that any decision about marriage would be my decision and mine alone. I tried again to explain about Lisa and that although we were very happy together we didn't have any immediate plans to marry. She looked a little sceptical. My brother and sister were both married and had children; my mother said her only desire was that I did the same before she died, or, as she put it, before she 'saw the road to God'. She wanted me to have someone to take care of me in this world, before she left it.

Both Kallu and Shekila said they would like to visit Australia at some point, although my mother felt too frail to make the journey. Shekila said she didn't need to see kangaroos or the Sydney Opera House, but she did want to see the house in which I was raised. They wanted to meet my Australian family, and told me they prayed for them every day at the mosque.

One of the most touching things my mother said to me was that if I ever wanted to come back to live in India she would build me a home and go out and work hard so that I could be happy. Of course, my intention was the reverse: I wanted to give *her* a home and do everything I could to make her happy.

Money can be a tricky subject in families, but I wanted to share the good fortune I'd had. By the standards of my Indian family, I was a wealthy man, with an annual salary they could only dream of. But I was aware that I had to tread carefully, because I didn't want the issue of money to complicate or taint our new relationships.

The four of us discussed what arrangements would be of most benefit. My mother's new work as a house cleaner earned about 1200 rupees a month – a much greater sum than she earned when I was little, but still a pittance, even in the context of regional India. We worked out a way for me to supplement her income. When I told my siblings I wanted to buy my mother a house, we discussed whether she might leave Ganesh Talai, and live closer to Shekila or Kallu. But she was happy where she was, and wanted to stay in the neighbourhood she had lived in all her life. So we resolved to find her something there, possibly even the place she was in now, but with much-needed repairs.

Inevitably, the subject of my father came up. My brother and sister were both completely unforgiving of him. They didn't doubt he would have seen the publicity surrounding my return, but were adamant they'd turn him away if he appeared, however contrite he was. He had abandoned us when we were children and needed his help, and they felt he had to live with the decision he'd made. They also blamed him for the loss of Guddu – if he hadn't left us, Guddu wouldn't have been forced into his dangerous work on the railways. In their view, the lines of fate went back from Guddu's death and my disappearance to the day that my father brought his new woman into our home and presented her to our then-pregnant mother.

But although my family had sworn they would never have anything to do with him again, no matter what the circumstances, I couldn't find it in myself to feel the same. If he regretted his behaviour, then I could forgive him. Perhaps because I'd also made a decision that spiralled out of my control, I could imagine that he might have made a bad decision, and everything else had rolled on from that. I couldn't hate him for making mistakes. He remained my father – even if I didn't really know him – and couldn't help but feel that my reunion with my past was incomplete without him playing a part.

I had always had doubts he would be interested in seeing me, but towards the end of my stay, I received word from someone who was still in touch with him. He had indeed heard the reports of my return and had been angry that no-one in the family had contacted him. He had recently been unwell and wanted to see me. The message captured my dilemma almost perfectly – despite the unsympathetic tone, I couldn't entirely harden my heart against him in his illness. However, there wasn't time to go to Bhopal, let alone raise the question with the family and seek their blessing. It was something I would have to let go for the time being.

Someone I had been eager to meet for a long time was Rochak, a local lawyer in his twenties who was the administrator of the Facebook group 'Khandwa: My Home Town'. He visited me at the hotel and it was nice finally to put a face to the name. His group had been absolutely crucial in confirming I had found the right place. Rochak had also helped me work out the best way to travel to Khandwa from where I sat at my computer in Hobart. Facebook had helped lead me back to my family as much as Google Earth.

I was pleased to be able to thank Rochak in person. He was genuinely delighted at the role he and his Facebook friends had played in my story, confirming details like the location of the fountain and cinema near Khandwa Station (once he had realised the cinema I was referring to had closed down). Unfortunately, he forgot at the time to send me some photos to confirm it, and I hadn't pressed him. Now, Rochak said he realised he could have been more helpful had he known why I was asking – I'd been nervous and coy about telling anyone what I was up to.

Rochak was out of town when the story of my homecoming broke, but he quickly worked out what had happened when he came back to find his that Khandwa Facebook group suddenly had 150 new members, half of whom not only didn't live in Khandwa but weren't even Indians.

He liked the way the internet was putting people in far-flung regional places like Khandwa in touch with others around the world, as it was expanding people's horizons and building relationships that once would have been impossible. Some people deride Facebook relationships and say you should get real friends in the real world. Rochak helped me online in the most profound way – surely there is no better basis for friendship.

Before he left, Rochak reminded me of the Hindu saying 'Everything is written': destiny takes its inevitable path. He thought my finding my home and family was a fulfilment of destiny, as was his helping me.

Rochak had also helped me in one final way, by organising a car and driver to take me on the hour and a half trip to Burhanpur, where I was to stay the night before embarking on a journey with painful memories.

I had a train to catch.

13

RETURNING

There was one more thing I felt I had to do before I could put to rest some of the ghosts of my past. I wanted to go back to Kolkata as an adult, and to get there I would take a train from Burhanpur, just as I'd done as an imprisoned, panicked five-year-old, and see what memories it brought back.

In India, there is no such thing as simply making a rail booking. With the immense pressure on limited seats, a booking has to be certified beyond any possible challenge to ensure that when you get on that train there is no-one already sitting in your seat and that it is yours for the entire journey. This is made all the more difficult when you don't really know where you're going – I needed some help to work out what train it might have been that took me across the country.

I had first met Swarnima at the Khandwa station, having just abandoned a long queue at the ticket window when I realised that speaking no Hindi was going to make it difficult to be sure I was getting what I needed. I had been feeling a bit defeated by the whole process, so her help was invaluable. Trains only go north-east or south-west out of Burhanpur, and together we worked out that both directions provided a possible route to Kolkata – one involved going south to Bhusawal, a more significant rail hub, from which there was a line heading roughly east across the country, and the other meant heading north-east before eventually arcing south-east towards the West Bengal capital. The northerly journey could be made without changing trains.

When I was being shown the two routes I might have been taken on twenty-five years earlier, I had to face up to the uncertainty of a few elements of my memories of that time. I had clearly been wrong about one important detail. I had always thought I had woken up on the train and arrived in Kolkata later the same day, having travelled roughly twelve to fifteen hours. That was what I'd always told everyone, and indeed, it was the basis for a lot of my searching on Google. But there was simply no way to get from Burhanpur to Kolkata in that time. It's a 1680-kilometre rail journey on the northerly route, and only a hundred kilometres less to go east via Bhusawal. The trip was going to take up to twenty-nine hours. I knew I got on the train in Burhanpur during the night, so I must have spent another night in transit. Maybe I slept through the entire second night. Or perhaps, as a terrified five-year-old, waking and sleeping between fits of panic and crying, I just lost track of how long it had been. Either way, it was clearly a longer journey than I had remembered.

This explained why my meticulous searching of Google Earth came to nothing for so long. Not only did I spend a long time looking in the wrong areas of the country, but even when I was looking west, the rough boundary I had calculated based on how far I might have gone in my imagined timeframe was much too close to Kolkata. I only found Burhanpur in the end by taking an incredibly fortuitous look outside my search boundary. Might I have found it more quickly if I'd got the time right? Perhaps, but perhaps not – as I'd decided that the only reliable method was to follow train lines out from Kolkata, I still would have spent a long time examining them, and I would have had to trace them further. I suppose once I'd exhausted my search zone, I would have widened it and kept going – I like to think I would have got there eventually.

As I wondered which of the two routes I should book a seat on, another long-held assumption was challenged. I had always been certain that after Guddu and I had jumped off our train,

I had slept on a bench, woken up to find a train in front of me and boarded it, all without moving from the platform. As we'd travelled south from Khandwa to Burhanpur, any train on the same line would almost certainly have also been heading south, and you can't get to Kolkata that way without changing trains. I had to concede that either I was wrong about not moving from the platform where Guddu left me – in which case I might well have boarded a northbound train and been spirited directly to Kolkata – or I went south and at some point changed trains.

As I've mentioned, my memories of that frightful night are not entirely clear and sometimes I feel there are things I've only dimly remembered. Occasionally, I get flashes of them – so although my most prominent memory is that once I was on the train I was unable to escape it, I do have a disjointed, fragmentary image of the train at a station, and me getting off it and jumping on another train. This is a flicker in the back of my mind, quite separate from my memories of the train ride, and I'm uncertain of it. But could it mean I initially made the trip south and then – because the train ended its service or I realised I was heading the wrong way – I switched trains to try to get back? It was possible, and that meant I might have reached Bhusawal and accidentally boarded an eastbound service to Kolkata.

Once the chance of my having changed trains was factored in, there was no way of determining which of the two routes I was most likely to have taken. A switch at Bhusawal might have sent me snaking east, but I might also have successfully switched to a train heading back north towards Burhanpur, then slept through the stop and been dragged off on the north-east route to Kolkata. Perhaps the southbound train I originally boarded itself turned back north at some point while I slept, or maybe the carriage I was on was transferred to another engine, which did the same. I had to concede I was unlikely to ever work it out – it would remain a mystery.

I felt that if I couldn't know for certain I was retracing my trip exactly, then maybe which route I chose didn't really matter – the point was to travel the distance and get a sense of the immensity of the journey, and perhaps to shake loose some more buried memories or put some things to rest. With that in mind, I thought I'd stick with my main memory of being trapped aboard for the duration and take the most direct, north-easterly path. If I'm honest, it was also partly because it was the easiest to organise and the most comfortable – there was a service that left Burhanpur at dawn, whereas the southerly route required further travel to Bhusawal late at night and waiting until the wee hours for a train headed east.

The train I decided I would take, then, was the Kolkata

Mail, which had plied the same route in the Eighties, when it was known as the Calcutta Mail. It started in Mumbai, on India's west coast, and reached Burhanpur at 5.20 a.m. – which is why I needed to be there overnight – before making its way to its namesake eastern capital. In fact, this particular service wasn't very likely to be the one I boarded as a child, even if I did somehow end up on the north-easterly route. It was scheduled to stop at Burhanpur Station for just two minutes, during which time a conductor would check off the names of the new passengers. How could I have jumped on and fallen asleep before it left the station? And I know there was no conductor around back then; indeed it's a mystery how I didn't see one during my entire ordeal. Conductors are a regular presence on interstate trains, which is one of the reasons I couldn't get far out of Kolkata when I was trying to find the way back: because I was avoiding conductors, I was probably unwittingly boarding only local trains. (There was an element of luck in this: if I had succeeded in leaving Kolkata, the chances were strong that, rather than being taken to Madhya Pradesh, I would have ended up somewhere else again, amplifying the problem. I could have been doubly, then trebly lost. Outside Kolkata, I was unlikely to have been found by an adoption agency.)

I didn't want thoughts about retracing my steps exactly to complicate things further. So, having chosen the Kolkata Mail, with the help of Rochak and Swarnima everything was put in place. When the car to Burhanpur arrived, I set off for a final visit to my mother. By this time, Swarnima had returned to work in Pune, where she lived, but fortunately Cheryl was able to help with our last few minutes of conversation over a parting cup of chai. We posed for family photographs together; looking at those photos now, I find it striking how much I resemble my mother and siblings.

My mother and Cheryl accompanied me out to the car, and we passed a crowd of curious locals who'd gathered to watch the lost boy take his leave from his family again. This was an especially wrenching departure – we were re-enacting the day I got lost. The last time I'd left on this particular journey, as a child, I hadn't said goodbye; now, a quarter of a century later, my mother hugged me tightly, smiling all the while. Although it must have been as emotional for her as it was for me – even more so – this time she wasn't worried that I wouldn't come back. She knew that now we would always find each other.

I spent the evening in the courtyard restaurant of my hotel in Burhanpur, watching the last skyrockets of people's Diwali stockpiles light up the sky. I knew taking the Kolkata Mail wouldn't solve all the mysteries of my original journey. In fact, I was nervous at the prospect of the trip, and of which other memories – recollections that have been the cornerstone of my identity – it might challenge.

I'd been told it was a good idea to get to Burhanpur Station an hour early to be on the safe side, so when I eventually turned in I set my alarm for ten past three in the morning. I needn't have bothered – a knock on my door woke me, and I opened it to a young man in a military jacket, his face almost entirely obscured by a headscarf, who identified himself as an autorickshaw driver booked for me by the hotel desk. The hotel had no hot water, so I woke myself up with a jet of cold water and just on four o'clock checked out and stepped into the darkness outside. We loaded my luggage into the three-wheeler auto and zoomed off down silent streets, past new blocks of flats, fully built, half-built and, according to the many colourful billboards, coming soon. I saw these signs all over India, each one boasting a new building with a gym, pool and all the mod cons, which I guess reflected the economic boom.

It was cool before the sun rose. I had barely slept from the anticipation of my journey, so the cooler air was a welcome help in keeping awake. Around us, I saw silhouettes of cows sleeping under awnings and pigs huddled together.

We pulled up outside the station, where a few people sat

around in groups and others slept on the ground, blankets pulled up to cover them entirely, which made them look unsettlingly like they were in body bags. Inside, a brightly lit red sign told me the train was an hour late. So much for my careful planning.

I had ample time to look around the station from which my first journey to Kolkata had begun. Even though it felt much the same place as I remembered it, some things had changed. I recalled the platform benches being made with wooden slats, including the one I slept on that night. Now the seats were of polished granite within a wooden frame. Also, while Ganesh Talai seemed much filthier now than when I was little, back then the Burhanpur station had been dirty and full of litter but now was very clean. On the wall there was a poster of a police officer nabbing a man spitting on the platform.

Looking across to the opposite platform, I felt sure it was the one that I'd boarded from, trying to find Guddu. I simply must have travelled south initially, even if I somehow came back through Burhanpur for the northern route. My head swam with all the possible permutations.

A chai man plying his trade on the other platform noticed me looking over and caught my attention. With little else to do, I waved to him that, yes, I'd welcome a cup. He gestured at me to stay where I was, then jumped down and crossed the tracks, balancing my cup on his metal tray. Just as he'd clambered back onto his platform, a freight train came thundering through the station – an awesome, frightening spectacle. In Australia trains tend to slow down at stations, but here, massive trains hurtled through at regular intervals, shaking the platform. The chai man lived with these trains and judged his timing expertly, but how much harder it would be to make those judgements if you were distracted, by grief or guilt. And I couldn't help imagining what would happen if you made a mistake. Was that what had happened to Guddu?

Despite the confusion about which platform I'd boarded from and whether I'd stayed aboard a single train, I still have clear, if disjointed, images in my head of the train journey itself. Clambering aboard and looking for Guddu, then curling up on one of the seats and going back to sleep. Wakening to bright daylight in an empty carriage, hurtling along. I have some memory of the train stopping at least one point along its route, with no-one around, but of always being unable to open any of the doors to the outside. I was confused and frightened, and I suppose it's not surprising I didn't keep a good track of time. It must have felt an eternity to a child of that age.

By small degrees daylight came, and people were still arriving at the platform in dribs and drabs – it seemed that the train's late arrival was predictable. Some were wrapped up as if the temperature was below freezing – in such a hot place, the dawn cool could be uncomfortable for the locals. They hefted all manner of suitcases, bags and bundles, and domestic appliances taped up tightly in cardboard cartons. As the light strengthened I saw the big water tower behind the station, which had helped me identify Burhanpur from the sky. I was lucky it hadn't been knocked down or moved, or I wouldn't have recognised the place.

The Kolkata Mail slipped into the station as dawn arrived. It had already travelled 500 kilometres in eight hours northeast from Mumbai, on the Arabian Sea. I stood at the point at which my assigned carriage was to draw up and, sure enough, a conductor consulted his list before ushering me onto the carriage, where I found my allocated seat. I didn't plan on doing things quite as hard as I had the first time around – I'd booked a 'first-class compartment', which I'll admit I hoped would be like the Orient Express as per Agatha Christie, but it fell a little short. There were no luxury carriages on this train, or staff in starched white uniforms with gold buttons offering gin and tonics on silver trays. The configuration of the carriages was very similar to the low-class one I'd boarded as a child: sets of single seats facing each other at the window, and across the aisle a sort of open compartment of facing bench seats, which could be used for sleeping. The appointments in this class were better, of course, but the worn maroon leather seats were still quite hard. Fortunately I wouldn't have to sit for the whole journey. My ticket also bought me one of the bench bunks across the aisle, and, at least for the time being, I had the area to myself.

It's another mystery that my recollection of my first journey is of my carriage being empty from the first time I woke until its arrival in Kolkata. An empty train carriage in India is unheard of, yet I am certain it was – I would surely have asked anyone who got on for help, even a conductor. There may have been people travelling in the adjacent carriages, of course, and I wouldn't have known – I didn't see or hear anyone else. I remained sitting in my empty carriage, waiting for someone to open a door. Was the carriage locked up and being hauled off for repair? Did I somehow end up on a works train, not meant for passengers, and not a scheduled service at all? If so, why would it have gone all the way to Kolkata?

As the train started to inch away from the platform, I shivered, remembering how this moment had begun the process of my getting hopelessly lost. But I was here to set something right, by confronting the fear I'd had, the circumstances back then, and travelling the distance again as a more comprehending, capable adult. I was also returning to Kolkata, to see again the places where I'd survived on the streets, and to visit Mrs Sood and the others at Nava Jeevan, the place where my fortunes had taken a dramatic turn. As the train picked up speed and cleared the Burhanpur platform, I looked around the carriage and wondered what personal journeys my fellow passengers were making.

When I was a child, air travel in India was for only the most important people: politicians, business moguls and their families, or Bollywood film stars. The railways were the veins of the country, circulating goods, people and money. Trains brought glimpses of the more affluent city life to our backwater town in the middle of rural India. It's not surprising that we spent a lot of time hanging around railway stations watching people come and go, making whatever money we could by selling things to passengers – as Guddu did with the toothbrush and toothpaste packs that got him arrested – or begging for whatever they might give us. The railways were our only connection with the rest of the country, and for most people that's probably still the case.

They aren't terribly fast, though. When Swarnima and I booked the Kolkata Mail I learned that it averaged fifty to sixty kilometres an hour. My Indian college friends had overestimated typical train speeds somewhat, which was lucky, as it made my original search field larger than it ought to have been, based on my faulty recollection of a half-day trip. Had they known how slow the trains were, it might have taken me longer to get around to searching further afield. I settled back in my seat, with nearly thirty hours of travel ahead of me.

At first, most of my fellow passengers kept to their cabin bunks, catching up on sleep. But eventually people could be heard moving around and murmuring, before curtains were drawn back to reveal travelling families waking up and facing the day.

We had travelled for just over an hour when I experienced a poignant moment. If it was this north-eastern route I had been on as a child, I would have passed through my home town, Khandwa. I knew we were headed there, of course, but rolling into town just as it was coming to life for the day's activity, inevitably made me wonder if I'd done this before, as a sleeping five-year-old. Had I awakened there, I might well have had the opportunity to get off the train and simply go home, presuming Guddu had met some friends or found something he needed to do. I could have climbed into my own bed, disappointed I hadn't got to stay away with him for longer. And then none of the things that followed – my experiences on the streets in Kolkata, my rescue and my adoption – would have occurred. I would not be Australian, and you would not be reading my story. Instead, perhaps I slept through a two-minute stop at Khandwa, not far from where my mother and sister were probably asleep themselves, and was borne away from what would have been a very different life.

As thoughts like these trailed through my mind, the day got underway and the sounds on the train became louder. Each voice had to be pitched to overcome the rumbling and clattering of the train on the tracks. Everybody seemed to have a mobile phone, all blaring with ringtones of popular songs from Hindi films, and there was constant conversation. In the background was what sounded like a compilation CD of many different styles of contemporary Hindi music, including jazz and even what seemed to be Hindi yodelling. Wallahs began their regular trips up and down the carriage, selling food and drink with a sort of chant: 'Chai, chai, brek-fist, brek-fist, om-lit, om-lit.'

Stretching my legs on a little walk, I found the pantry car, where cooks stripped to the waist fried huge quantities of chickpea and lentil snacks in boiling oil, and boiled mountains of sliced potato in vast vats. The vats and pots rested on bricks and were heated by enormous jets of gas, and the cooks tended them with long wooden paddles – it was amazing to watch them do all this on a bumpy train.

There weren't any carriages on the Kolkata Mail like the one I'd been trapped in, with barred windows and the rows of hard wooden benches. You also couldn't walk between the carriages on that train – they only opened onto the platform, and didn't have interconnecting doors. It seemed more and more likely that on my first trip, I'd been in some sort of carriage that wasn't in use – the bustle and noise of an Indian train are inescapable, and the chance that the carriage would otherwise have remained empty was nil.

As we travelled north-east, the landscape we passed through was as I remembered it: flat, dusty and seemingly endless, although this time I was composed enough to see some of the texture and details of the place: expanses of cotton and wheat fields, irrigated crops and chilli plants with so many chillis on them they looked red from a distance, as well as the usual cows, goats, donkeys, horses, pigs and dogs. Combine harvesters worked side by side with bullocks and carts, and farmers harvested by hand, building piles of hay. There were villages of tiny brick and plaster houses painted in pastel colours like pale pink, lime green and faded sky blue, with old roofs of terracotta tiles that looked like they could fall off at any moment. We also passed through tiny railway stations painted in the brick-red, yellow and white patterns of Indian Railways. I must have seen a few of these when I hurtled along back then, begging the train to stop at one. I wondered whether anyone in these fields looked up at a passing train and saw a small face at the window, looking out with fright.

I thought about Kolkata, and found that I was more excited than anxious. Even though parts of it would be full of memories, it would also be like visiting a place for the first time. I was lost in Calcutta, but I was returning to Kolkata. Both of us had changed, and I was looking forward to seeing how much.

Night had begun to descend as I had these thoughts, and by the time I'd folded the seat down and unpacked the Indian Railways linen from its paper covering it was dark. I lay down on my bunk, and found I could still see out the window to watch the lit-up temples, bicycle lights and house lights flash by as the train rolled on.

With the train's bumping and swaying, an unexpected sense of wellbeing came over me. I felt at ease lying there, bouncing along in my bunk amid the chatter of people speaking in languages that sounded familiar but which I didn't understand. During the day, I'd had a chat with a curious little boy from the next open compartment. He was about ten years old and keen to try out his school English, with 'What's your name?' and 'Where are you from?' He seemed to be able to tell that I was not from India, despite my looks – maybe it was my clothes, or that I didn't join in conversations in Hindi or Bengali. When I told him I was from Australia, he mentioned Shane Warne. After talking about cricket for a bit, he asked me, 'Are you married?' When I said I wasn't, he told me how disappointed he was for me. 'Who are your family?' he asked next, and I found myself hesitating. 'My family live in Tasmania, but I also have family here, in Khandwa, in Madhya Pradesh,' I said at last. That seemed to satisfy him, and I realised that it had also begun to satisfy me.

Late in the morning of the next day, we began the approach to Kolkata. From the vantage point of the train, I could watch how the tracks we were on merged with many others, so there came to be numerous sets of rails in parallel, running into Howrah Station. I might have travelled these lines as a boy, but who knows? I might not have managed to get on any that came out to this western edge of the city. There seemed to be an impossible number of lines, which could take a person in every possible direction. I was seeing the evidence that I'd never stood a chance of finding my way back.

The train seemed to speed up now, passing through level crossings where trucks and cars and autorickshaws waited, with everyone blasting their horn. It wasn't long before we were deep in one of the world's biggest cities, along with somewhere between 15 and 20 million other people. It was 12.20 p.m., exactly thirty hours after my departure from Burhanpur, when the train coasted into the massive, red-brick Howrah Railway

Station, which gave me tingles of recognition as we inched up to the platform and stopped. I had returned.

When I got off the train, I took a minute or two to simply stand in the middle of the busy station concourse and let the crowd rush by me, just as I did back then. This time people surged around me, as they would any adult standing in their way, whereas last time I had stood here, pleading for help, I don't think they even saw me. On the one hand, I believed that among all those people there wasn't one willing to take the time to help a lost child. On the other, I wondered whether any other reaction was possible – in a crowd this size, everyone was anonymous, invisible. Why would one upset kid be of any particular interest amid all the activity of the place? And if anyone stopped, how much patience would they have had for being mumbled at in Hindi about a place they'd never heard of?

The station building itself was hauntingly familiar. I'd begged in it, slept in and around it, and spent those weeks making futile train trips to try to get out of it. It had been my home at a most traumatic time of my life. But now it was just a train station, albeit a very big one, and busier than any I'd ever seen. There wasn't much to gain from hanging around, when I didn't have to.

I didn't notice any homeless children inside – perhaps they were more likely to be moved on these days – but I did see a couple of small groups once I walked outside the building into the brutally strong sun. They had that unmistakable look about them: grubby from street living, and somehow simultaneously idle and alive to opportunities, such as someone passing close by from whom they might beg or perhaps steal. Could I have ever found myself a gang, or had I been too wary or naïve? It's hard to imagine I could have survived the streets on my own for much longer than I did. I would have been one of these kids, or dead.

I found a taxi. Before long, I was heading to the hotel my travel agent had booked, which turned out to be quite upmarket, with Indian and Western food, bars, a gym and an infinity pool. I went for a swim: at the pool you could lounge around on recliner chairs on the pool deck, or swim over to the infinity edge and look out at Kolkata, many floors down and extending as far as the eye could see, along with its smog, traffic chaos and poverty.

One of the main reasons I'd come to Kolkata was to meet someone who'd played an absolutely central part in my life. Once I had learned that Mrs Saroj Sood was not only still alive, but still working for ISSA, I'd made arrangements to visit her in her office. Now I linked up with my Bengali translator and took a taxi through the mad traffic, dust and stink of untreated sewage.

The ISSA office was in a rundown Victorian building in Kolkata's Park Street quarter, an area with many restaurants and bars, and the Flurys tearoom, which people visit for the famous cucumber sandwiches and cake. Amid all this highlife and refinement, it's a centre of salvation.

We passed through an outer office, where staff at desks worked through large stacks of papers. Then I saw her, scrutinising a computer monitor and surrounded by official-looking files in the cramped inner office, an old air conditioner stuck hazardously onto the wall above her – Mrs Sood. The place looked exactly as it had twenty-five years before.

Mrs Sood's eyes widened when I walked in and introduced myself. We shook hands and embraced. She was now in her eighties, but she said she remembered me well from when I was a child, despite the number of children who had passed through her care since then. 'I remember your mischievous grin. Your face has not changed,' she told me, in her excellent English, smiling widely. We had last seen each other in Hobart, a few years after my adoption, when she had arrived escorting another adoptee.

She asked me about both of my mothers and then asked a social worker she worked with, Soumeta Medhora, to find my adoption file. While they talked about where it might be,

I looked at the pin-up boards on the walls, covered with pictures of smiling children.

Mrs Sood had been working to help children in need in this same office for thirty-seven years. In that time, she had arranged adoptions for around 2000 Indian children, some to families in India and others to families overseas. She also had a daughter of her own, a successful businesswoman who told people that she had 'donated her mother' to the work of adoption.

Born in Delhi, Mrs Sood gained a law degree and became interested in adoption. She arranged her first adoption within India in 1963, and three years later succeeded in assisting a Swedish exchange student, Madeleine Kats, to adopt an Indian girl in Sweden. Kats became a journalist, and when she wrote of her experience, mentioning Mrs Sood, other people from abroad started asking for help arranging an adoption. And so it all began.

Mrs Sood moved to Calcutta, receiving training from the Missionaries of Charity, the order that Mother Teresa founded; indeed, she was blessed by Mother Teresa herself. She gained some other influential patrons – the president of the All India Women's Conference, and a renowned Independence freedom fighter, Ashoka Gupta – and with their support registered ISSA in 1975. Seven years later, the organisation set up the orphanage I stayed in, Nava Jeevan, meaning 'new life'.

Mrs Sood told me that my adoption had gone through

easily, especially compared to the average international adoption today. She said that intercountry adoption was now managed by a central authority, rather than directly through agencies like ISSA, but that measures designed to 'streamline' procedures had instead made the process ever more complicated and lengthy. It now commonly took a year, and sometimes as long as five years, for all the paperwork, arrangements and procedures to be finalised. I could feel her frustration, and I knew that Mum felt the same way – she had become a passionate advocate for making international adoption easier, after going through the delays in adopting Mantosh, and seeing how the extra time in adverse circumstances had affected him.

In 1987, Mum and Dad, having received approval for adoption, met with an ISSA staff member escorting adoptees to Australia, who showed them my file. They immediately agreed they would take me. Two weeks later Mrs Sood visited them herself, on a trip to escort my fellow Nava Jeevan adoptees Abdul and Musa, and brought back the photo book my new parents had prepared for me.

I asked Mrs Sood whether it was unusual for families abroad who adopted an Indian child to adopt a second, even if they were not related. She said it was quite common – the first child would get lonely, or culturally isolated, or the parents just enjoyed the experience so much they wanted to repeat it.

Tea was brought and while we drank it together, Mrs Medhora returned with my file and I was able to see the actual documents of my adoption. The pages seemed a little faded and fragile, almost as if they could fall apart at a touch. Attached to the file was a photograph of me in Australia, which my parents had sent after I arrived. I was grinning and holding a golf club, standing in front of an old-fashioned golf buggy. There was also a photocopy of my passport, with its photograph of the six-year-old me looking steadily into the camera. My official documents and passport all had my name as 'Saru', which is how it had been recorded since I arrived in the police station. It was Mum and Dad who had decided 'Saroo' was a more anglicised spelling, more like it sounded.

The file revealed that I had come to the attention of the authorities in Calcutta after I was accepted into the custody of officers at Ultadanga Police Station on 21 April 1987. I was assessed and taken to Liluah, the juvenile home, where I was classified as a child in need of care. There were two other categories for children at Liluah – those whose parents had come to the attention of the police and courts, and those who themselves had committed offences – and we were all bunked in together.

The picture of what happened to me then became a little clearer. I had been in Liluah for one month and then given into the care of ISSA at a hearing in the Juvenile Court on 22 May.

Mrs Sood would regularly visit Liluah to ask about new admissions needing care and, where appropriate, she would apply to the court to have them handed over temporarily to ISSA. Her agency was given two months to find the child's family and reunite them or to have an orphaned child declared 'free' to be adopted into a new family. If unsuccessful, the child would have to return and remain in Liluah, although ISSA could continue to pursue their case. This was Mantosh's fate, as it took ISSA two years to untangle the difficulties within his family and have him released for adoption.

In my case, staff at ISSA took a photo of me – the first I'd ever had taken – and it was published on 11 June in a Bengali daily newspaper with a notification that I was a lost child. On 19 June they published it in the *Oriya Daily*, a widely read newspaper published in the state of Orissa (now known as Odisha), because they thought I might have boarded the train in the coastal city of Brahmapur. Of course, there was no response – it was miles away from where I actually lived. I was therefore officially declared a 'neglected child' and was formally made 'free' for adoption, after my agreement, on 26 June.

My case for adoption by the Brierleys came up for hearing on 24 August and was approved – so I was in Nava Jeevan for two months. I was issued with a passport on 14 September, departed India on 24 September and arrived in Melbourne the following day, 25 September 1987. From the moment the teen-ager with the handcart had taken me into the police station until the moment I stepped off the aircraft in Melbourne, the entire process had taken only a little over five months. Mrs Sood said that if I was being adopted now, the process would take years.

Mrs Medhora corrected a misconception I'd had about how I had come to be chosen for release from Liluah, which I thought was because I had been in good health. The real rea-son was because I'd been lost – ISSA's first intention had been to reunite me with my parents. Children with disabilities of all kinds were released from Liluah, if it was thought there was a possibility they could be reunited with their families. Soon after my adoption went through, ISSA had managed to reunite with their families two other lost children who'd been in Liluah after advertising in the newspapers. But I'd just had too little infor-mation for them to start a meaningful search.

In fact, they didn't even know that I'd spent some weeks on the streets of Kolkata. Confused and no doubt a little fright-ened about what was happening to me, I'd just answered the questions that were put to me. And even if they'd asked me directly about it, I probably wouldn't have been able to tell them much – I was poor and uneducated, and my language was too limited to be able to communicate much. ISSA had only learned that I'd been on the streets years later, when Mum told them after she'd learned about it from me. Mrs Sood said they had been astounded. Most couldn't imagine a five-year-old from a small town surviving on the streets of Kolkata alone for a few days, let alone several weeks. I had been incredibly lucky.

After Mrs Sood and I had said our fond goodbyes, and I'd thanked her again for everything she'd done for me, a driver took Mrs Medhora, my interpreter and me down yet more congested roads, past a new metro train line under construction, to a quiet residential street of apartment blocks in the northern suburbs, looking for Nava Jeevan. In fact, the orphanage had moved, and the building I knew was now used as a free daycare centre for children of poor working mothers.

At first I was convinced we'd come to the wrong place. Mrs Medhora tried to reassure me, but I was so certain of my memories, I thought she must have become confused with all the moving the orphanage had done over the years. It turned out I didn't recognise the second storey of the building because I'd never been in it – toddlers lived downstairs and babies upstairs.

When I went into the downstairs quarters, I found the Nava Jeevan I remembered. There were a dozen or so young children taking their afternoon nap, stretched out on mats on the floor. These kids, though, were collected by their mother and taken home at the end of the day.

Two more places to visit remained. Firstly, we went to the

Juvenile Court in which I was pronounced an orphan, in a suburban satellite town oddly named Salt Lake City, about half an hour's drive from central Kolkata. It was a dingy, nondescript building, and I didn't stay there long, on either visit. The second, though, was Liluah Home. Given my less than happy experiences there, it had promised to be a confronting visit, which I think was why I'd left it till last. I hadn't exactly been looking forward to seeing it again, though I knew my visit to the Kolkata of my childhood wouldn't be complete without it.

Once again ISSA kindly provided a car and driver, and we crossed the landmark Howrah Bridge and went past Howrah Station, threading our way through narrow alleyways to reach the imposing building – almost a fortress. As the car pulled up outside, I saw again the massive red rusted gates that I had never forgotten, with the small hatchway entrance to one side, just like a prison. The gate was immense in my childhood memory, and was still imposing now. The high brick walls were topped with metal spikes and jagged glass.

By now, as the blue sign over the entrance informed me, it had become a Home for Girls and Women. Boys were sent elsewhere. Although it looked the same, and there were still guards on duty outside, it felt a little less brutal somehow – perhaps it was just that this time I was here as a visitor.

Mrs Medhora had arranged for us to be admitted, so we

went straight through a little doorway. Inside, we came across a large pond that I barely remembered being there. The buildings appeared smaller and much less menacing than they had. But something about the atmosphere still made it feel like a place you would want to get out of as soon as possible.

We made a tour and I saw the same kinds of bunk-lined halls in which I had slept and dreamed of release. I would never have imagined when I left here that I would one day willingly return, yet here I was now, looking over the place, a tourist of my old terrors. But, more than any other visit I made, Liluah put the pain of that past somewhat to rest at last. After all, what alternatives did the authorities have in dealing with lost and abandoned children? They put them somewhere they tried to make safe, and gave them food and shelter while they tried to find a place for them. Of course these homes weren't set up with the intention of making kids' lives miserable, or for preying on them. But when you put that many kids together, some of them much older than others and some of them violent, bullying is inevitable and abuse is possible, even likely.

And if you don't have the resources to secure the boundary properly, then your best intentions become corrupted. I thought about the way outsiders had breached what looked like a fortress, and I wondered how that could have happened without someone turning a blind eye. No doubt, there needed to be stricter controls in place to avoid such blights on the system. I felt more than thankful that I had survived my stay there, and got out relatively unscathed.

There was one last visit I had to make – not a particular building, but an area. On my final day in Kolkata I returned to the streets near Howrah Station, and the little group of cheap cafes and shops that still clung to the top of the banks of the Hooghly River. It remained a place for the less well-off, workers on a pittance, homeless people. There was still no sanitation, and a lot of people lived in makeshift lean-tos and stalls in the area. I walked around the shop stalls, recalling how I used to smell the mouth-watering fruits and fried foods on sale here, and marvelled that I had been able to detect them at all over the stench of human waste mingled with diesel and petrol fumes, and smoke from cooking fires.

I walked down to look at the river's edge, but the area between the shops and the water seemed to have been divided up into private housing plots. Just as I was trying to work out a way through, several mangy-looking dogs came my way up a little alley, nosing past my legs, and I decided I didn't want to put my anti-rabies shot to the test. Instead, I took the footpath away from the row of shops to the impressive steel span of the Howrah Bridge, and before long joined the stream of people at the start of its pedestrian walkway, which links the city of Howrah with central Kolkata. When I first crossed it, I was escaping my terrifying experience with the men from the railway shack. Now I knew the bridge was a major Kolkata landmark, probably the best known in the city. It was one of the last major British projects before India achieved independence, in 1947.

The massed humanity crossing it, and the stream of vehicles of all kinds, were incredible. People pushed behind me and rushed towards me. Bearers moved to and from the railway station like ants walking to and from their nest, with astonishingly bulky loads balanced perfectly on their heads. Beggars lined the railing along the walkway, raising their steel bowls and shortened limbs, and adding their chants to the boisterous noise of the bridge. The scale of human presence and activity almost made the bridge a neighbourhood in itself. But the crowds also started to make me feel insignificant, as though I didn't exist. How small I must have felt when I crossed it as a little kid.

The traffic noise was tremendous and there were clouds of blue smoke rising, momentarily cloaking the scene. I'd read that living with the air pollution even of Sydney or Melbourne can reduce your lifespan, so I could only wonder by how much your life would be shortened here, breathing in this kind of pollution, day in, day out.

Around a third of the way across the bridge, I stopped at the railing and looked back at the riverbank, to a place below the station and the shops, the area where I had somehow survived as a boy. Now there was a ferry jetty in the place I remembered walking along, and underneath the bridge the bank had been concreted. I couldn't see if the sadhus could still sleep there. I hadn't seen many sadhus during my return visits to India, but I didn't know if theirs was a lifestyle in decline or if it was just coincidental. They'd felt like guardians to me when I'd slept near them or their shrines.

I looked down at the stone steps – the *ghats* – that led into the powerful tidal waters of the Hooghly, at the place where I had almost drowned, twice, and thought about the man who had plucked me from the water both times. He would almost certainly be dead by now. But, like the teenager who later took me to the police station, he had given me another chance to live. He hadn't profited from his act in any way – unless he was a believer in karma – and I had never thanked him. I was too embarrassed and frightened by the attention when he pulled me out the second time. So as I stood there at the railing looking down at my past, I thanked that man, and then I thanked him again, as the sun began to set and my last day in Kolkata ended in a smoky, pink-grey haze.

It was time to go home.

EPILOGUE

The moment of my two mothers meeting for the first time was an incredible milestone. When the idea of filming their introduction had been floated by *60 Minutes*, to be featured as the centrepiece of a story about my experiences, I found myself once again apprehensive. There always seemed to be another emotional journey ahead of me yet to be travelled. Would Mum feel somehow less bonded to me when she met the woman who had given birth to me? Would she worry that Kamla, my mother, might demand my return? Would Kamla find it impossible to connect with Mum, or feel awkward about being thrust together with her in front of the cameras? I knew Mum was nervous about that, as well as about what would amazingly be her first visit to India.

Of course, I always wanted to bring my two families together, and they had all spoken of looking forward to such a meeting. Despite finding the prospect a little daunting, I was disappointed my dad wasn't able to join us this time. For now, it was to be my mothers laying eyes on each other for the first time.

When the moment arrived in Ganesh Talai, with the *60 Minutes* crew in tow, time seemed to stand still. All concerns washed away as I watched my mothers – who had given me not just one life, but two – embracing with tears in their eyes. How many events since I was a little boy had lined up to lead to this day? It was staggering.

We communicated through a translator, but the joy and love we shared didn't need much translation.

Mum greatly admired the strength of Kamla in surviving the many struggles of her life. It gives me great pleasure to be able to help my mother in India however I can, including taking care of her rent and buying food – whatever might make things more comfortable for her. Typically, she resists, insisting that all she cares about is having me back in her life. Despite her soft protests, now that I have secured the dual citizenship that permits me to buy property within India, I plan to buy her a better home in Ganesh Talai, nearby to her friends. Patience is required when doing business in the poor village, and I'm waiting on the paperwork, but Kallu, Shekila and I have found Kamla a place just around the corner from where she waited for me all this time. We all look forward to helping her move into her own home – her first.

I am also devoting time to helping another incredibly important woman in my life, without whom I would be unlikely to be here to write my story: Saroj Sood. I am assisting with repairs to the Nava Jeevan orphanage for abandoned babies and lost children. Words can't properly express my gratitude to Mrs Sood and her dedicated staff at ISSA. If I can help her with her mission to care for children who find themselves in situations similar to that which befell me, I will do everything I can.

My desires for myself are less clear. Even as I poured all my efforts into tracking down my home town and family, I was never searching in the hope of somehow getting back to the life I had missed. It wasn't a matter of needing to right a wrong, nor one of wanting to return to where I belong. I grew up almost all of my life in Australia, and I have family bonds here that cannot be challenged or broken. I wanted to know where I came from – to be able to look at a map and point to the place where I was born – and to throw light on some of the circumstances of my past. Most of all, though I tried to keep my expectations in check as insurance against disappointment, I hoped to find my Indian family so they would know what had happened to me. My bonds with them can never be broken, either, and I am deeply grateful that I now have the opportunity to renew our connection.

But I am not conflicted about who I am or where to call home. I now have two families, not two identities. I am Saroo Brierley.

Nonetheless, revisiting India and seeing the lives of my siblings and my mother has been a culturally enriching experience as well as a personal one. I look at my brother and sister, particularly, and admire their traditional focus on family and relationships. It is difficult to put in words, but I feel that perhaps there is something in the West we have lost in our impersonal suburbs and emphasis on individualism. I am not a religious person, and cannot imagine that changing, but I am keen to learn more about the customs and beliefs of my Indian family, and to see if they offer some guidance for me.

I am also delighted to have met my niece and nephews, and I look forward to being a part of their lives and to provide them with whatever opportunities I am able.

Had I not become lost – not gone out that night with Guddu, or somehow found my way home soon after – my life would have been hugely different, of course. Much suffering would have been avoided. My family would not have endured the heartbreak of a missing son, on top of the tragic death of another, and I would not have known the pain of separation, and the cold fear that struck me in the train or on the Kolkata streets. But my experiences have undoubtedly shaped me, providing me with an unshakeable faith in the importance of family – however it is formed – a belief in the goodness of people and of the importance of grasping opportunities when they are presented. I wouldn't wish to erase any of that. It's true, too, that my Indian family received opportunities they would not have, had none of this taken place. I feel strongly in a sense of destiny about these events, intertwining my two families, with me as the linchpin.

I know my Mum and Dad wouldn't wish for their lives to have been different, without me and Mantosh. I am unspeakably grateful to them for the love – and the life – they have given me, and I have nothing but admiration for their commitment to helping others less fortunate. I am confident that my finding my Indian home will bring my Australian family closer together, rather than making anyone question our connection.

When I told Mantosh that I had found my family, he was naturally very happy for me. Some news of his sadly fractured family has filtered through to us from ISSA and Mantosh has found my success in reuniting with my Indian family inspiring. Despite the painful memories of his childhood, and his struggles growing up, he has renewed his interest in trying to reconnect with his Indian mother. We're not sure if it is possible, but I would like nothing more than to see my brother achieve some of the peace of mind granted to me.

I was also delighted to celebrate my good fortune with Asra, my friend since our time together at Nava Jeevan and our mutual, eye-opening journey to Australia. In the early years, with our families having become firm friends, we kept in touch by phone quite often, and occasionally visited each other's homes interstate. Although we lost touch a little as we got older, as people do, we still catch up every now and then, with news of jobs, relationships and life in general. There are some aspects of my experiences that only Asra and I can share, and I consider myself lucky for having such a friend.

When I look back to the process of my rediscovering Khandwa – the Google Earth searches that consumed me, in particular – I realise that I could have approached things differently, and might possibly have found what I was looking for more quickly. I could have been more forensic about the various 'Burhanpur'-type towns and cities that appeared on maps and thought to consider those further across the country from Kolkata. It's possible that deeper internet searches might have ruled out some of these places straight away, or at least narrowed the field. I might also have restricted my searches to train lines near a shortlist of 'B' towns, rather than pedantically tracing all routes out from Howrah Station to a roughly calculated perimeter, even if there was a juggernaut logic to my methods. Perhaps that would have delivered Khandwa more quickly, perhaps not.

But I didn't do it those ways – I did it the best way I could think to at the time. I don't have any regrets about how things transpired, with the exception of my brother's tragic death. I am astonished at the miraculous turns in my story – my Mum's vision that led her to intercountry adoption, my Indian mother praying and seeing an image of me the day before we were reunited. Even the remarkable coincidence of finding myself at school in a place called Howrah. It is sometimes difficult not to imagine some forces at work that are beyond my understanding. While I don't have any urge to convert that into religious belief, I feel strongly that from my being a little lost boy with no family to becoming a man with two, everything was meant to happen just the way it happened. And I am profoundly humbled by that thought.

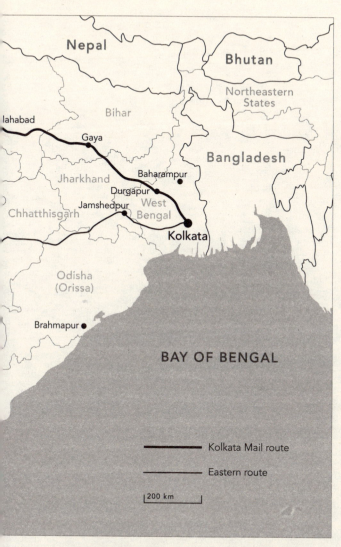

My Journey Across India
The two most likely rail routes from Burhanpur to Kolkata (assuming only one train change, or perhaps none), although I will never know for certain which was the one I was taken on as a child. No-one suspected I had been transported so far, which cruelled all efforts to find my home and family. In 2012, I rode the Kolkata Mail, crossing the country in much greater comfort.

ACKNOWLEDGEMENTS

I offer my deep gratitude to both my families for allowing me to tell their stories as part of mine, and for their openhearted support and assistance in the production of this book. I also thank Lisa for her love and patience during the process.

I am indebted to Saroj Sood for her contribution to my life as well as her help with the book, and to Soumeta Medhora. I would also like to thank Cheryl and Rochak for the help they provided, and especially Swarnima for being so giving of her time and for her friendship.

Finally, I would like to thank Andrew Fraser at Sunstar Entertainment for his guidance, Larry Buttrose, and Ben Ball and Michael Nolan at Penguin.

He just wanted a decent book to read ...

Not too much to ask, is it? It was in 1935 when Allen Lane, Managing Director of Bodley Head Publishers, stood on a platform at Exeter railway station looking for something good to read on his journey back to London. His choice was limited to popular magazines and poor-quality paperbacks – the same choice faced every day by the vast majority of readers, few of whom could afford hardbacks. Lane's disappointment and subsequent anger at the range of books generally available led him to found a company – and change the world.

'We believed in the existence in this country of a vast reading public for intelligent books at a low price, and staked everything on it'
Sir Allen Lane, 1902–1970, founder of Penguin Books

The quality paperback had arrived – and not just in bookshops. Lane was adamant that his Penguins should appear in chain stores and tobacconists, and should cost no more than a packet of cigarettes.

Reading habits (and cigarette prices) have changed since 1935, but Penguin still believes in publishing the best books for everybody to enjoy. We still believe that good design costs no more than bad design, and we still believe that quality books published passionately and responsibly make the world a better place.

So wherever you see the little bird – whether it's on a piece of prize-winning literary fiction or a celebrity autobiography, political tour de force or historical masterpiece, a serial-killer thriller, reference book, world classic or a piece of pure escapism – you can bet that it represents the very best that the genre has to offer.

Whatever you like to read – trust Penguin.